Google™ ILLUSTRATED

ESSENTIALS

Elizabeth Eisner Reding

COURSE TECHNOLOGY
CENGAGE Learning™

Australia • Brazil • Japan • Korea • Mexico • Singapore • Spain • United Kingdom • United States

COURSE TECHNOLOGY
CENGAGE Learning™

Google™—Illustrated Essentials
Elizabeth Eisner Reding

Executive Editor: Marjorie Hunt
Senior Product Manager: Christina Kling Garrett
Associate Product Manager: Rebecca Padrick
Editorial Assistant: Michelle Camisa
Marketing Director: Cheryl Costantini
Marketing Manager: Ryan DeGrote
Product Marketing Specialist: Jennifer Hankin
Developmental Editor: Karen Stevens
Senior Content Project Manager: Jill Braiewa
Art Director: Kun-Tee Chang
Print Buyer: Fola Orekoya
Text Designer: Joseph Lee, Black Fish Design
Copy Editor: Mary Kemper
Proofreader: Chris Clark
Indexer: Alexandra Nickerson
QA Reviewer: John Freitas
Cover Artist: Mark Hunt
Compositor: GEX Publishing Services

ISBN-13: 978-1-4239-9953-9
ISBN-10: 1-4239-9953-3

Course Technology
25 Thomson Place
Boston, MA 02210
USA

Cengage Learning is a leading provider of customized learning solutions with office locations around the globe, including Singapore, the United Kingdom, Australia, Mexico, Brazil, and Japan. Locate your local office at: **international.cengage.com/region**

Cengage Learning products are represented in Canada by Nelson Education, Ltd.

For your course and learning solutions, visit **course.cengage.com**

Purchase any of our products at your local college store or at our preferred online store **www.ichapters.com**

A-31: © MANSMANS

Printed in the United States of America
1 2 3 4 5 6 7 14 13 12 11 10 09 08

About This Book

Welcome to *Google™—Illustrated Essentials*! Since the first book in the Illustrated Series was published in 1994, millions of students have used various Illustrated texts to master software skills and learn computer concepts. We are proud to bring you this brand new Illustrated book that covers the latest Google tools.

Using the Google search engine to find information is a basic skill that millions of people apply every day. But most people only know the very basics of using Google search tools; they don't know how to take advantage of all Google tools that can help solve problems and increase productivity. This book is designed to expose students to the many tools that Google provides, and explain the benefits for using them. And, of course it also provides step-by-step instructions for learning each featured skill.

This book's unique design, which presents each skill on two facing pages, makes it easy for novices to absorb and understand new skills, and also makes it easy for more experienced computer users to progress through the lessons quickly, with minimal reading required. We hope you enjoy exploring some of the great tools that Google has to offer!

Author Acknowledgments

Elizabeth Eisner Reding I would like to take this opportunity to thank all those involved in the preparation and completion of this book. This project represents a slight departure from those in the Illustrated series in that it doesn't quite fit into any existing category.

Necessitated by the ever-changing landscape of Google products, this project required extreme flexibility as we broke old rules and created new ones. Thanks to Christina Kling-Garrett and Marjorie Hunt for hammering out the do's and don'ts of this project and making it a reality, and to Karen Stevens for the day-to-day administrivia of developing each unit and getting it finished. Thanks also to my husband, Michael, for his continual support, to Jeff Schwartz for his patience while content changed from one day to the next, and to Michelle Camisa, Jill Braiewa, Patricia Shogren, and everyone at GEX.

Preface

Welcome to *Google™—Illustrated Essentials.* If this is your first experience with the Illustrated series, you'll see that this book has a unique design: each skill is presented on two facing pages, with steps on the left and screens on the right. The layout makes it easy to digest a skill without having to read a lot of text and flip pages to see an illustration.

This book is an ideal learning tool for a wide range of learners—the rookies will find the clean design easy to follow and focused with only essential information presented, and the hotshots will appreciate being able to move quickly through the lessons to find the information they need without reading a lot of text. The design also makes this a great reference after the course is over! See the illustration on the right to learn more about the pedagogical and design elements of a typical lesson.

Key Features

Each two-page lesson is structured consistently to make it easy to learn a skill. Here are the key elements you'll find in every lesson.

- **Introductory Paragraph**—Each lesson begins with an introduction that provides an overview of a particular Google tool as well as its URL.
- **Why It's Important**—This section describes in more detail how each tool can be used to enhance your productivity and how it can be used to make you more effective.
- **Hands-On Steps**—Each lesson features a set of steps for completing a key task related to the lesson.

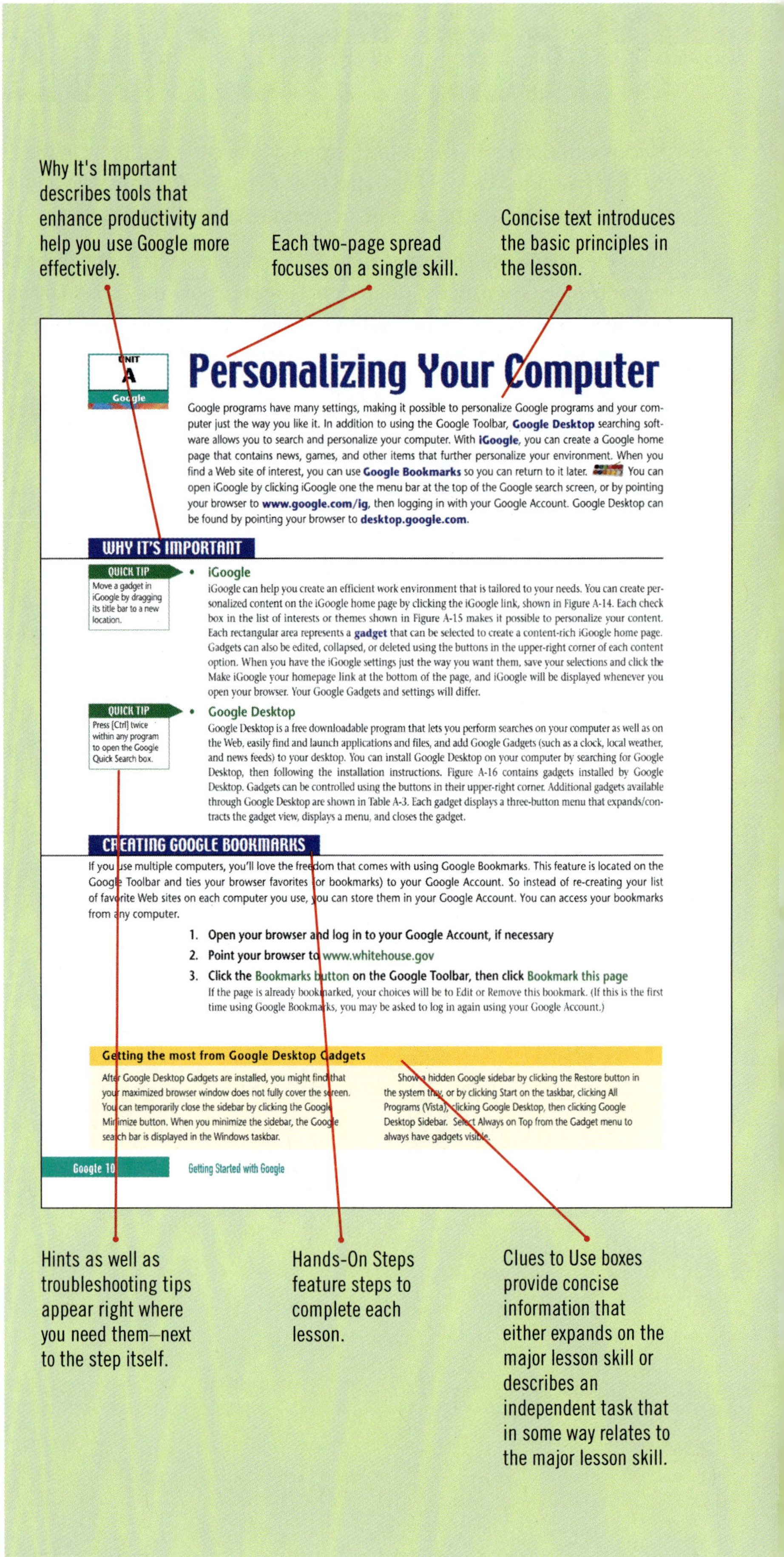

Every lesson features large, full-color representations of what the screen should look like as students complete the numbered steps.

FIGURE A-14: iGoogle link

FIGURE A-15: Personalize iGoogle settings

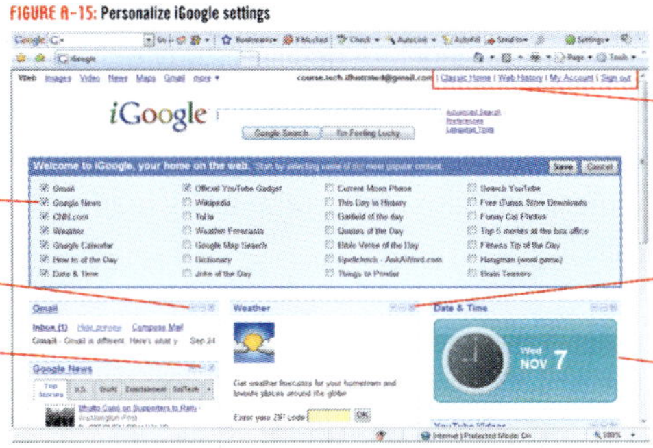

FIGURE A-16: Google Desktop Gadgets

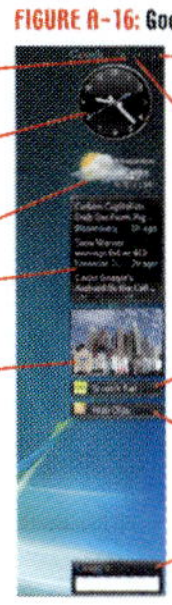

TABLE A-2: Some Google Desktop Gadgets

name	name	name
Art of the Day	Currency Converter	Technology News
Baseball News	Google Calendar	Temperature Converter
Best Flights Travel Search	Music Player	Ticket Finder
Best-Selling Books Space News	Package Tracking	TicketsNow
Clock	Star Trek Trivia	Website monitor

Google

Getting Started with Google Google 11

Tables provide summaries of key terms, buttons, or keyboard shortcuts connected with the lesson material.

Assignments

The assignments on the light purple pages at the end of each unit increase in difficulty. Additional case studies provide a variety of interesting and relevant exercises for students to practice skills.

Assignments include:

- **Concepts Reviews** consist of multiple choice, matching, and screen identification questions.
- **Independent Challenges** are case projects requiring critical thinking and application of the unit skills.
- **Visual Workshops** are practical, self-graded capstone projects that require independent problem solving.

Instructor Resources

The Instructor Resources CD is Course Technology's way of putting the resources and information needed to teach and learn effectively into your hands. With an integrated array of teaching and learning tools that offer you and your students a broad range of technology-based instructional options, we believe this CD represents the highest quality and most cutting-edge resources available to instructors today. Many of these resources are available at *www.course.com*. The resources available with this book are:

- **Instructor's Manual**—Available as an electronic file, the Instructor's Manual includes detailed lecture topics with teaching tips for each unit.
- **Sample Syllabus**—Prepare and customize your course easily using this sample course outline.
- **PowerPoint Presentations**—Each unit has a corresponding PowerPoint presentation that you can use in lecture, distribute to your students, or customize to suit your course.
- **Figure Files**—The figures in the text are provided on the Instructor Resources CD to help you illustrate key topics or concepts. You can create traditional overhead transparencies by printing the figure files. Or you can create electronic slide shows by using the figures in a presentation program such as PowerPoint.
- **Solutions to Exercises**—Solutions to Exercises provide a document outlining the solutions for the end-of-unit Concepts Review, and Independent Challenges.
- **ExamView**—ExamView is a powerful testing software package that allows you to create and administer printed, computer (LAN-based), and Internet exams. ExamView includes hundreds of questions that correspond to the topics covered in this text, enabling students to generate detailed study guides that include page references for further review. The computer-based and Internet testing components allow students to take exams at their computers, and also saves you time by grading each exam automatically.

CourseCasts–Learning on the Go. Always Available… Always Relevant.

Want to keep up with the latest technology trends relevant to you? Visit our site to find a library of podcasts, CourseCasts, featuring a "CourseCast of the Week," and download them to your mp3 player at *http://coursecasts.course.com*.

Our fast-paced world is driven by technology. You know because you're an active participant—always on the go, always keeping up with technological trends, and always learning new ways to embrace technology to power your life.

Ken Baldauf, a faculty member of the Florida State University Computer Science Department, is responsible for teaching technology classes to thousands of FSU students each year. He knows what you know; he knows what you want to learn. He's also an expert in the latest technology and will sort through and aggregate the most pertinent news and information so you can spend your time enjoying technology, rather than trying to figure it out.

Visit us at *http://coursecasts.course.com* to learn on the go!

COURSECASTS

Contents

Read This Before You Begin

This book was written as a guide to using Google products. Many people are accustomed to using Google to perform searches on the Internet, but are unfamiliar with some of the other products available bearing the Google brand. Due to the ever-changing landscape of Google products, an effort was made to keep steps as generic possible to prevent them from becoming outdated.

What software was used to write and test this book?

Although it is mentioned within the text, it bears repeating that Google products do not have to wait for specific product releases as with other popularly-available software products on the market. As such, the user can be confident in knowing that they are always using the most up-to-date version. Unfortunately, that makes the writing of an up-to-date text book analogous to changing a tire on a moving vehicle. *Please understand that when this book went to press, it was as accurate as humanly possible.*

Do I need to be connected to the Internet to complete the steps and exercises in this book?

Most of the exercises assume that your computer is connected to the Internet. If you are not connected to the Internet, see your Instructor or information on how to complete the exercises.

What do I do if my screen is different from the figures shown in this book?

This book was written and tested on computers with monitors set at a resolution of 1024 x 768 using a 4:3 aspect ratio. If the screen shows more or less information than the figures in the book, your monitor is probably set at a higher or lower resolution. If you don't see something on the screen, you might have to scroll down or up to see the object identified in the figures. If your screens contain different text, buttons, or links, it is possible that Google products have been updated since this book was published.

Are there any Data Files?

There are no Data files accompanying this text.

UNIT
A
Google

Getting Started with Google

Just about everyone has heard of Google, but you might not be aware of the depth and breadth of its offerings. Google products, from the Gmail Webmail service to Google Docs word processing program, are nearly all Web based, which means that you don't need to take up your computer's hard disk space storing Google applications. It also means that you can access your Google Account from any computer with an Internet connection. Because Google products are Web based, Google can update its software whenever updates are available, instead of waiting for a major release to issue a new version. In this unit, you will learn about Google products and how they can be used.

OBJECTIVES

- Learn about Google
- Understand Google search tools
- Search Google Images, Google Video, and Google News
- Use Google Maps and Google Earth
- Personalize your computer
- Collect information with Google Notebook
- Shop with Google Product Search
- Find your way using your phone
- Use Google help

Learning about Google

Google is an ever-growing collection of products designed to enhance your online experience and increase your productivity. A **Google Account** is free (you'll learn how to get one in this lesson) and having one means you can access any Google program from any computer with an Internet connection. Table A-1 lists the names of some commonly used Google products and their uses. Google search, and other commonly used Google products, can be reached by pointing your browser to **www.google.com**.

WHY IT'S IMPORTANT

QUICK TIP
If you already see the Google Toolbar, you can click the Google button to go to the Google search screen. If you don't have the Google Toolbar, you'll learn how to get it in the next lesson.

- **Search the Web**
  When you type **www.google.com** on the address line of your browser, shown in Figure A-1, the classic Google search screen opens. From this screen, you can access the nearly limitless possibilities of the Web. Whatever your interest, you can probably find information on it using the search screen. Whether it's research for the most important meeting of your professional life, or the hobby that soaks up all your free time, this is your starting place. You might already see a Google Toolbar or Search text box in your computer's browser. This additional feature lets you conduct searches *without having to open the Google search screen.*
- **Communicate with others**
  Google has a wide variety of tools you can use to communicate with others, including sending and receiving e-mail, chatting online, and scheduling appointments. You can use Google Groups to create forums of other users and Blogger to create ongoing threads of communication on specific topics.
- **Share images and video**
  Images you take with a digital camera or videos you take with a digital camcorder, or images you acquire elsewhere, can be manipulated and sent to other users using a variety of methods. You can use Google to share images with friends and family, regardless of whether they have a high-speed Internet connection or access to a digital camera.

QUICK TIP
Google products are very intuitive. Links are provided on product pages to answer any questions you might have.

- **Enhance productivity**
  Screens in Google products are intuitive and easy to use, and many have a similar look and feel. Because its screens are largely text based, navigating the programs doesn't require memorizing a lot of cryptic icons. This means that rather than spending time learning how to use different products, you can be more productive almost immediately by using Google products, such as Google Desktop, Google Calendar, and Gmail. You can always get help when using any Google product by pointing your browser to **www.google.com/support**.

GETTING A GOOGLE ACCOUNT

If you have access to the Internet, you can create a Google Account. You don't need a Google Account to use Google search, but you will need one to personalize Google for your own tastes and to use the galaxy of Google options. Follow these steps to open a Google Account:

1. **Open your browser, type www.google.com in the address line, then press [Enter]**
2. **Click Sign in**
3. **If you don't have a Google Account, click Create an account now, as shown in Figure A-2, or if you already have an account, enter your Google Account e-mail and password**
4. **Fill in the required information, read the Terms of Service, then click the I accept. Create my account. button**
5. **Sign in with your Google Account**

FIGURE A-1: Google search screen

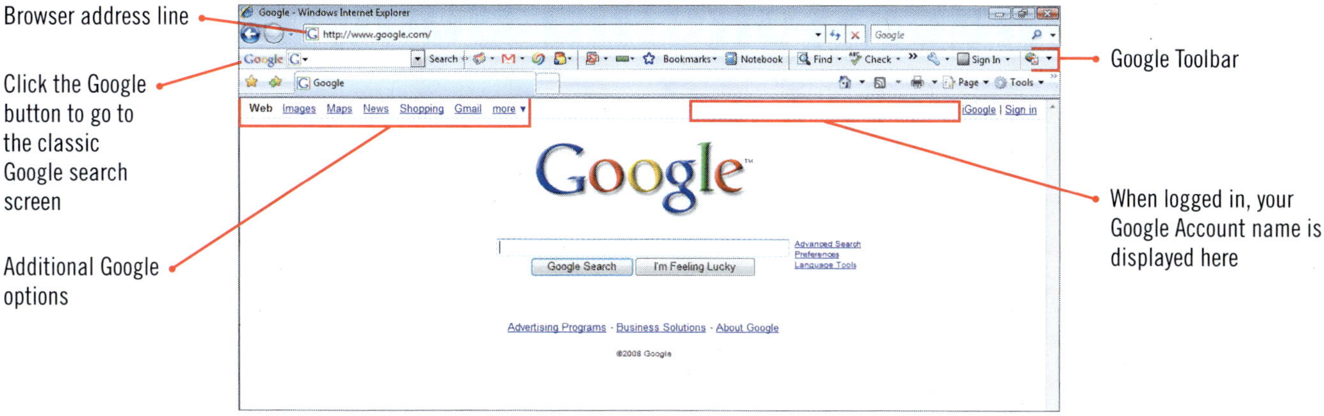

FIGURE A-2: Google sign in

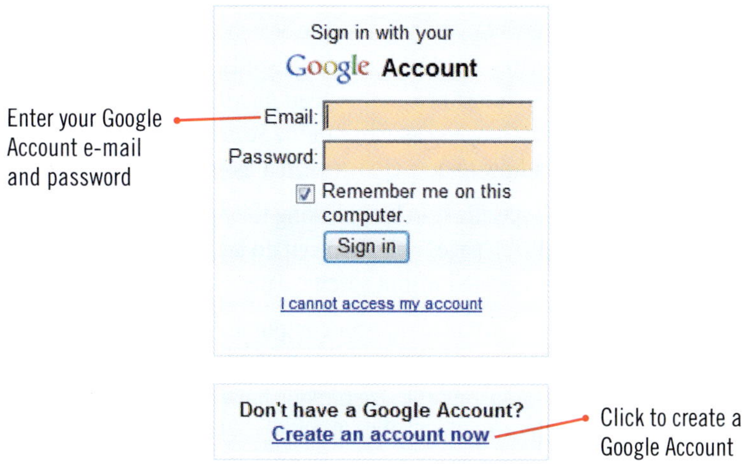

TABLE A-1: Commonly used Google programs, their uses, and their URLs

program	used to	Web address
Gmail	Create, receive, reply, and organize e-mail	*mail.google.com*
Google Alerts	Retrieve information of interest	*www.google.com/alerts*
Google Calendar	Create and track appointments	*www.google.com/calendar*
Google Catalogs	View online catalogs	*catalogs.google.com*
Google Desktop	Personalize your computer	*desktop.google.com*
Google Images	Search for images on the Web	*images.google.com*
Google Maps	Get directions	*maps.google.com*
Google Maps for Mobile	Download directions and traffic information to your phone	*www.google.com/mobile/gmm*
Google Mobile	Use Google products on your mobile device	*www.google.com/mobile*
Google Notebook	Store information on specific topics	*www.google.com/notebook*
Google Product Search	Shop with multiple online vendors	*www.google.com/products*
Google Talk	Send instant messages using your computer	*www.google.com/talk*
Google Toolbar	Add Google tools to browser	*toolbar.google.com*
Help	Support for Google programs	*www.google.com/support*
iGoogle	Web portal used as a home page	*www.google.com/ig*
Picasa	Organize, modify, and share images	*picasa.google.com*

UNIT A
Google

Understanding Google Search Tools

Performing a basic search sounds simple enough, but it opens the door to getting the most out of the Web. If you know how to conduct a search, your experience using the Web will be enriched. You can begin your search by using the classic Google search page (at www.google.com) or by using the **Google Toolbar** search bar, installed in your browser, from any Web page. Additional search techniques are listed in Table A-2.

Google search is available at **www.google.com**.

WHY IT'S IMPORTANT

QUICK TIP
If you click the I'm Feeling Lucky button, Google will automatically take you to the top-listed choice on the search results list.

QUICK TIP
You can enter a telephone number in the search text box to find out owner's name and address, and get a map.

- Knowing how to phrase what you enter in the Search text box is important. When you enter text in the Search text box, be specific, but brief. In other words, if you want information on National Parks, type *National Parks* in the Search text box, rather than *Information on National Parks*. If you are using the Google search screen, after you have typed an entry in the Search text box, press [Enter] or click Google Search. You can find out more about how to do a Google search using the Google Help Center, shown in Figure A-3.
- You can conduct a more specific search by clicking the Advanced Search link. This feature lets you search on specific variables to find Web pages written in certain languages, having some or all of the parameters you've requested, or Web pages updated within specific dates.
- After the Google Toolbar is installed on your computer, you can enter search criteria from any browser page; the Google home page doesn't have to be open. If the buttons on your toolbar differ from those shown, try reinstalling the toolbar, adjusting the size of your browser window, or changing your screen resolution. To conduct a Google search using the Google Toolbar, click the Enter query to search text box, then type your criteria. As you type, you'll see suggested results. When you see a suggestion that matches your interest, click the entry with your mouse, as shown in Figure A-4.
- With either method, a list of possible links for your topic will be displayed. Figure A-5 shows a list of results matching your search. You can click any of the links to find more information about your topic. At the bottom of the search page, you'll find a navigation bar that lets you advance to additional search results.

INSTALLING THE GOOGLE TOOLBAR

If you don't have the Google Toolbar installed on your computer, take a few moments to install it now:

1. **Open your browser and point it to toolbar.google.com**
2. **Click the Install Google Toolbar button (from Internet Explorer), or the Download Google Toolbar button (from Firefox), then follow the installation instructions**

TABLE A-2: Additional Google search techniques

to find pages about	enter the following in the search text box	explanation
A vacation in Germany	vacation Germany	the words you want information about
Belgium or Germany	Belgium OR Germany	words separated by uppercase 'OR'
The phrase 'to be or not to be'	"To be or not to be"	phrase separated by quotation marks
Binghamton University's nursing site	nursing site:www.binghamton.edu	URL preceded by '(optional: specific info) site:', 'link:', 'info:', or 'related:'

FIGURE A-3: Google Help Center

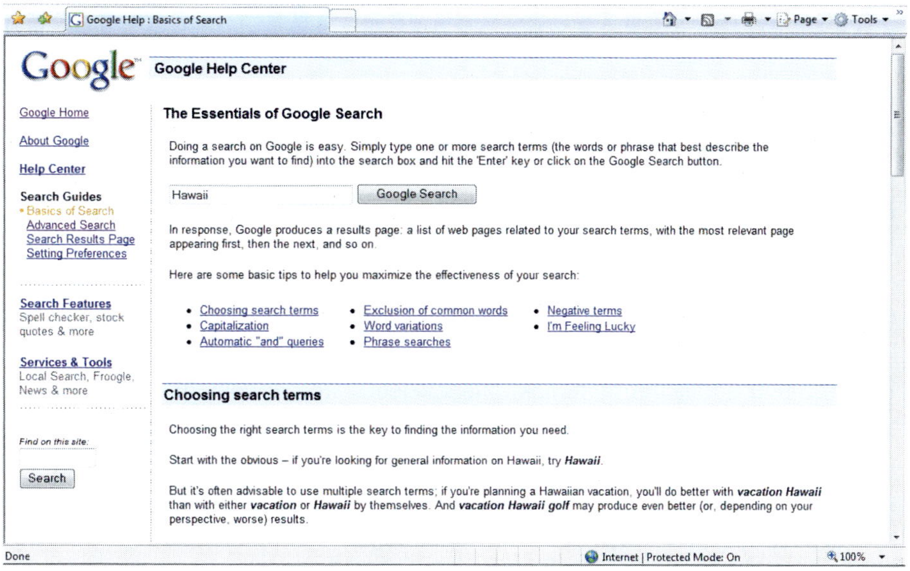

FIGURE A-4: Entering search criteria in Google Toolbar search bar

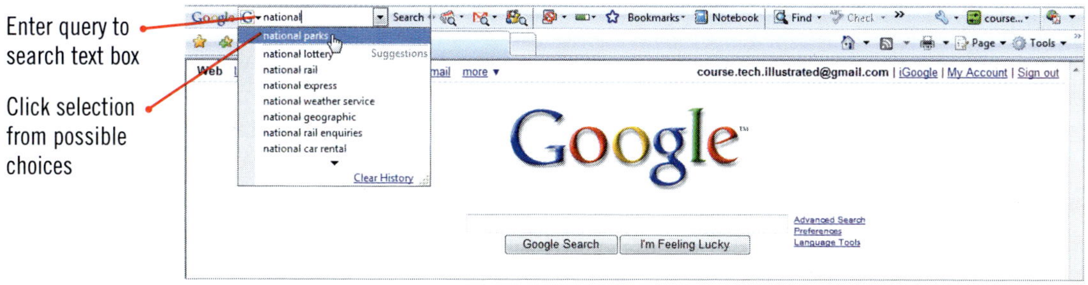

FIGURE A-5: Search results

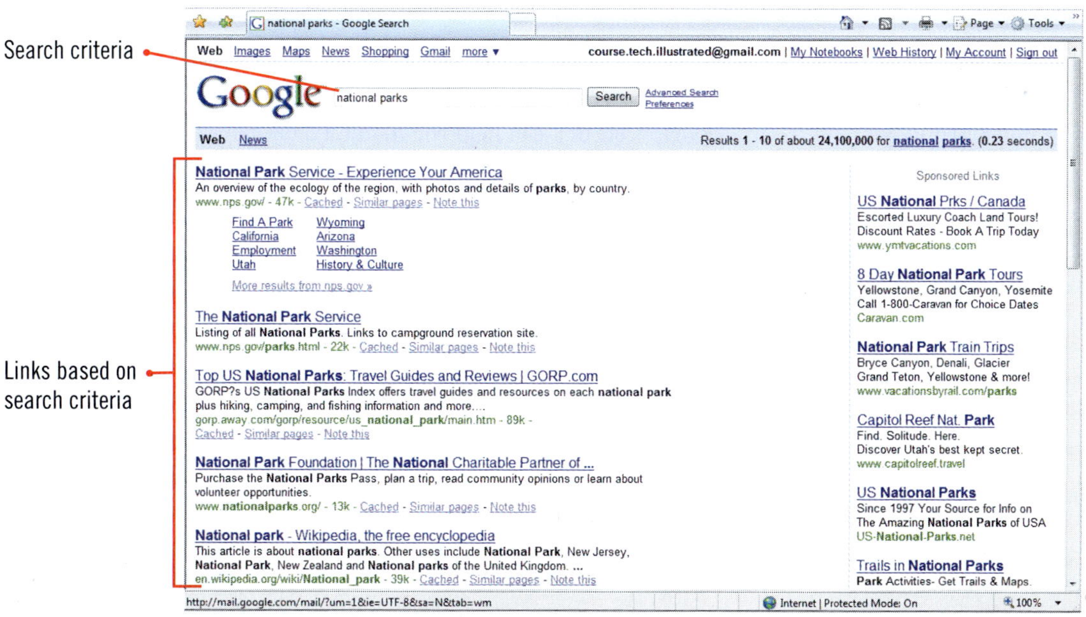

Searching with the Google Toolbar

Once installed, the Google Toolbar can make searching a breeze. When you type your search parameters, remember the following simple rules:

- search text is *not* case sensitive
- it is not necessary to include "and" between multiple terms
- it is not necessary to include common words such as "how" or "where" in search parameters

You can also use Google search to find definitions from multiple sources by typing define: *word*, then pressing [Enter].

UNIT
A
Google

Searching Google Images, Google Video, and Google News

At the top of each Google page is the list of available menu options, and additional menu options can be found by clicking the more link. The options for refining your search are images, maps, and news. **Google Video**, found under the more link, offers video search options grouped into categories such as Most blogged, Most shared, Most viewed, and Movers & Shakers. **Google News** news service provides up-to-the-minute news stories from a variety of sources on topics such as World, U.S., Business, Sci/Tech, Sports, and Entertainment. You can refine your searches by pointing your browser to **www.google.com**, then clicking the Images, News, or more links from the menu bar.

WHY IT'S IMPORTANT

QUICK TIP

When you download an image, make sure you consult the copy right information associated with that image. Just because you can download an image, doesn't mean you can use it without obtaining permission.

- **Images**

  Google Images images search lets you find imagery for almost any imaginable topic. With the existing search criteria still displayed, if you click Images in the menu bar, images of national parks are visible, as shown in Figure A-6. You can find out more about a particular image by clicking its thumbnail. Additional options are displayed by right-clicking the image thumbnail.

- **Video**

  View a variety of video clips on your search criteria by clicking more from the menu bar, then clicking the Video menu option. See Figure A-7. Your ability to view video might depend on your computer's hardware configuration.

- **News**

  When you click the News menu option, you'll see a wide variety of news stories, each listing the source and how recent the story is. Figure A-8 contains news listings for national parks. If there's a specific topic you are interested in, you can create a Google Alert that can help you monitor a developing news story. Alerts can search the Web, News, Blogs, Video, Groups, or all of these sources. You can choose to be alerted daily, as it happens, or weekly. To create an alert, point your browser to **www.google.com/alerts**.

TRACKING YOUR PAST WITH WEB HISTORY

Creating Web searches and following the resulting links can get overwhelming, and it's easy to get so wrapped up in what you're doing that you can forget where you've been. Don't worry if you lose track. Google has a Web History feature that makes it simple to retrace your steps:

1. **Open the Google search screen and log in to your Google Account, if necessary**
2. **Click the Web History link**

   You might have to reenter your password to access this feature. Figure A-9 shows time-stamped entries for recent searches. Your Web History results will differ.
3. **Click the link to return to a specific search item**

Staying Alert with Google Alerts

You can use **Google Alerts** e-mail update service to keep up-to-date on topical issues and events. To create an alert, point your browser to **www.google.com/alerts**, enter the search terms you want to monitor, pick the type of medium you want to monitor (News, Blogs, or Video, for example) and how often, then enter your e-mail address and click Create Alert.

FIGURE A-6: Images of national parks

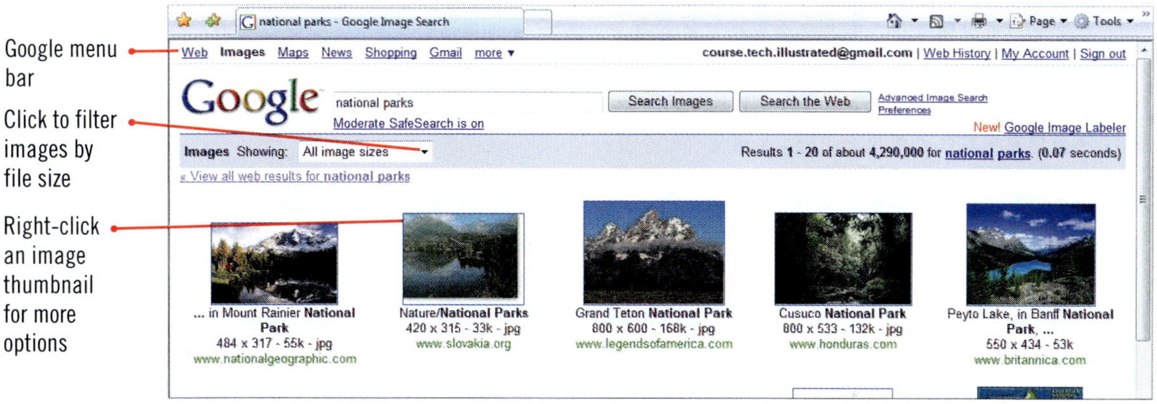

FIGURE A-7: National park video results

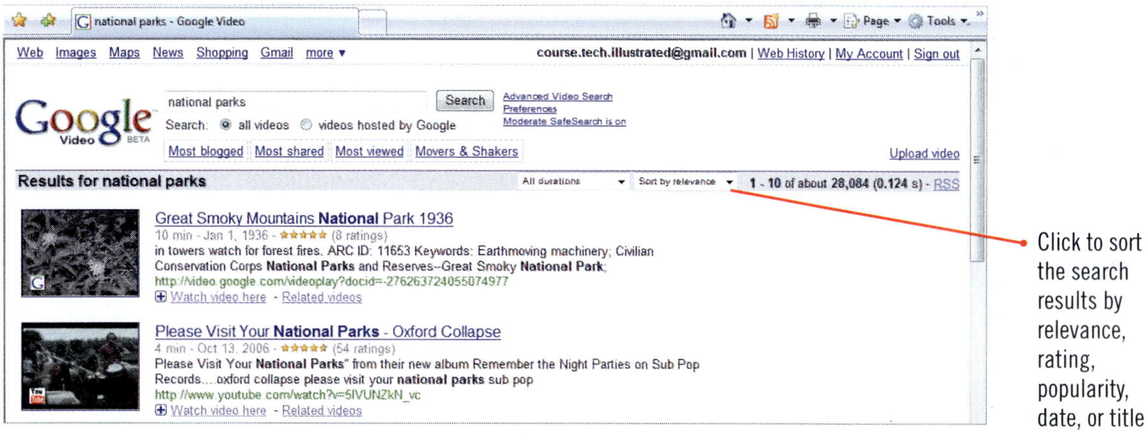

FIGURE A-8: National park news

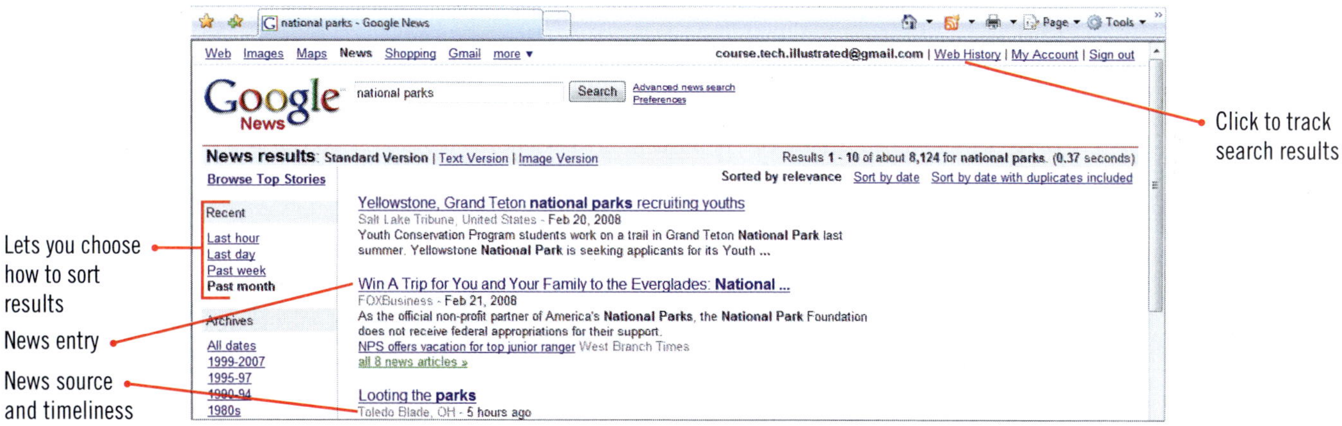

FIGURE A-9: Web History

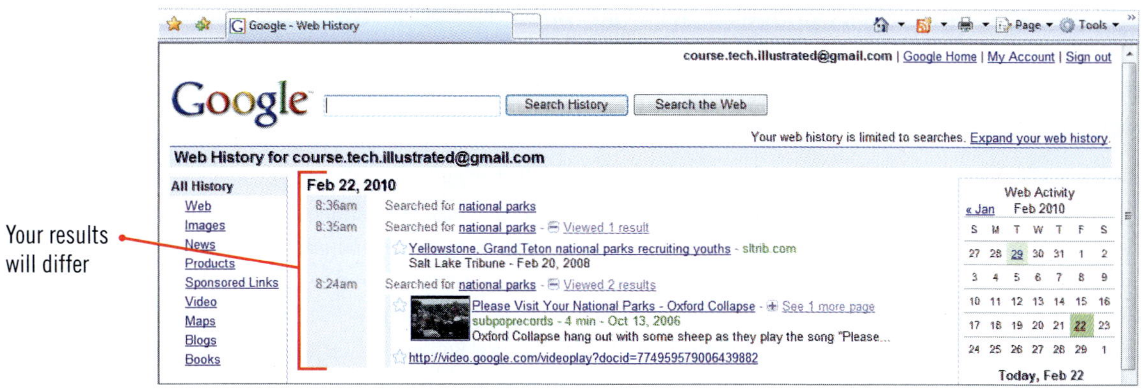

Using Google Maps and Google Earth

So you've done a search, seen images and videos, and read news on a specific topic. Now you're ready to use **Google Maps** mapping service, which offers street and satellite views that give you turn-by-turn instructions to help you get to your destination. Combining the power of the Google search engine with satellite imagery and mapping, **Google Earth** mapping service is a product that you can download and run from your desktop. You can open Google Maps by clicking Maps from the menu bar at the top of the Google search screen, or by pointing your browser to **maps.google.com**.

WHY IT'S IMPORTANT

QUICK TIP
You can use the panning buttons to change your view up, down, left, or right.

- **Google Maps**
  What could be more important than having accurate directions to get where you're going? With Google Maps, you can extend the power of the search one step further by saying "Okay, take me there." When you click the Maps menu option, Google Maps shows you a map indicating various points of interest that match your search terms. Click one of the points for additional details. Use the Get directions link and enter a starting point, and the map expands to give you detailed driving instructions. Click the Help link to open the Google Maps Help center, shown in Figure A-10. If you change your mind about the route, the starting and ending points on the map (as well as any other points on the route) can be dragged to a new destination. Once you've finished dragging any points, the map and the step-by-step directions are automatically updated.

QUICK TIP
You can add models to Google Earth with the 3-D modeling capabilities of Google Sketchup 6 at *sketchup.google.com*.

- **Google Earth**
  With Google Earth, you can utilize aerial and satellite imagery of the Earth from your desktop, as well as explore the stars, constellations, planets, and galaxies. Unlike a flat map, satellite imagery can give you a bird's-eye view of a specific area, so you can get a feel for the terrain. (If you don't already have Google Earth, you can download it by pointing your browser to **earth.google.com** or by searching for Google Earth, clicking the Download button, then following the installation instructions.) When you open Google Earth, the screen shown in Figure A-11 is displayed. Click the Product Tour link, shown in Figure A-12, to see how Google Earth works and view demos. One of the demos, shown in Figure A-13, shows you how to build 3D models.

SENDING GOOGLE MAPS TO YOUR PHONE

You can use Google Maps to send directions to a cellular phone:

1. **Create a Google search, open Google Maps, search for your desired destination, then click a link on the map**
2. **Click the Send to phone link**
3. **Type the cellular phone number (including 1 + area code) in the To text box**
4. **Select the cellular phone carrier from the Carrier list arrow**
5. **Click the Send button**

Be an explorer with Google Maps

When you look at Google Maps, you'll see several buttons across the top of the map. Each one of the buttons (Street View, Traffic, Map, Satellite, and Terrain) is a toggle that turns a feature on or off. Click the Street View button, for example, and the streets on the map become highlighted. Click the Traffic button and major traffic arteries are highlighted. (Not all buttons are available for all maps.) Did you know that anyone with a Google Account can make modifications to Google Maps? Some listings (such as hospitals) cannot be modified, but many mapped business locations can. Once you are logged into your Google Account, you can make modifications to business listings by clicking the Info for business owners link, then clicking the Local Business Center link.

FIGURE A-10: Google Maps Help Center

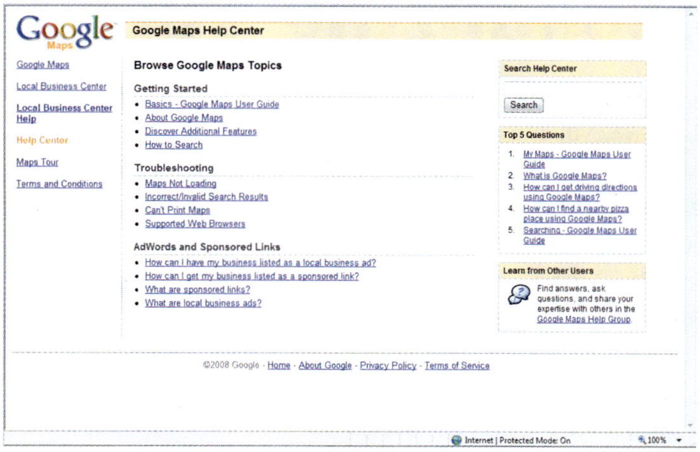

FIGURE A-11: Google Earth

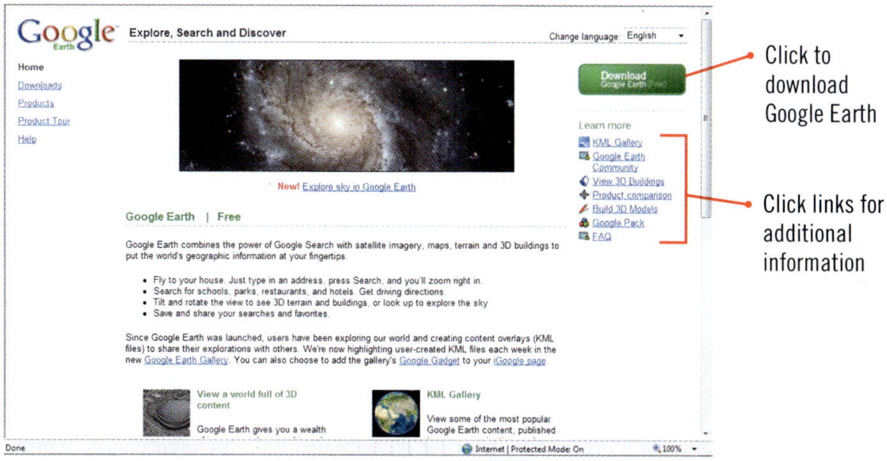

FIGURE A-12: Google Earth Product Tour

FIGURE A-13: Google SketchUp for building 3D models

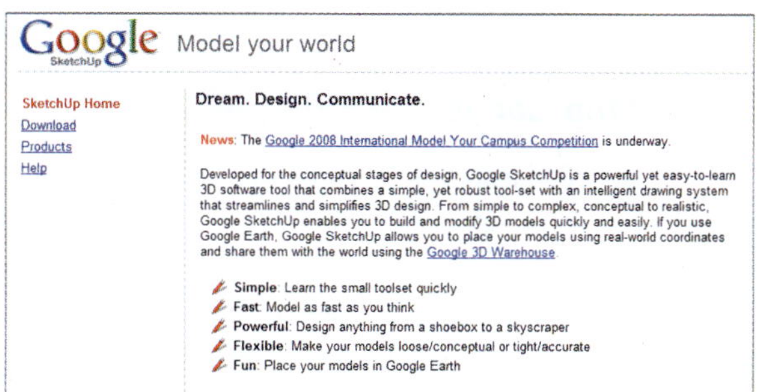

Personalizing Your Computer

Google programs have many settings, making it possible to personalize Google programs and your computer just the way you like it. In addition to using the Google Toolbar, **Google Desktop** searching software allows you to search and personalize your computer. With **iGoogle**, you can create a Google home page that contains news, games, and other items that further personalize your environment. When you find a Web site of interest, you can use **Google Bookmarks** so you can return to it later. You can open iGoogle by clicking iGoogle one the menu bar at the top of the Google search screen, or by pointing your browser to **www.google.com/ig**, then logging in with your Google Account. Google Desktop can be found by pointing your browser to **desktop.google.com**.

WHY IT'S IMPORTANT

QUICK TIP
Move a gadget in iGoogle by dragging its title bar to a new location.

- **iGoogle**
  iGoogle can help you create an efficient work environment that is tailored to your needs. You can create personalized content on the iGoogle home page by clicking the iGoogle link, shown in Figure A-14. Each check box in the list of interests or themes shown in Figure A-15 makes it possible to personalize your content. Each rectangular area represents a **gadget** that can be selected to create a content-rich iGoogle home page. Gadgets can also be edited, collapsed, or deleted using the buttons in the upper-right corner of each content option. When you have the iGoogle settings just the way you want them, save your selections and click the Make iGoogle your homepage link at the bottom of the page, and iGoogle will be displayed whenever you open your browser. Your Google Gadgets and settings will differ.

QUICK TIP
Press [Ctrl] twice within any program to open the Google Quick Search box.

- **Google Desktop**
  Google Desktop is a free downloadable program that lets you perform searches on your computer as well as on the Web, easily find and launch applications and files, and add Google Gadgets (such as a clock, local weather, and news feeds) to your desktop. You can install Google Desktop on your computer by searching for Google Desktop, then following the installation instructions. Figure A-16 contains gadgets installed by Google Desktop. Gadgets can be controlled using the buttons in their upper-right corner. Additional gadgets available through Google Desktop are shown in Table A-3. Each gadget displays a three-button menu that expands/contracts the gadget view, displays a menu, and closes the gadget.

CREATING GOOGLE BOOKMARKS

If you use multiple computers, you'll love the freedom that comes with using Google Bookmarks. This feature is located on the Google Toolbar and ties your browser favorites (or bookmarks) to your Google Account. So instead of re-creating your list of favorite Web sites on each computer you use, you can store them in your Google Account. You can access your bookmarks from any computer.

1. **Open your browser and log in to your Google Account, if necessary**
2. **Point your browser to www.whitehouse.gov**
3. **Click the Bookmarks button on the Google Toolbar, then click Bookmark this page**
   If the page is already bookmarked, your choices will be to Edit or Remove this bookmark. (If this is the first time using Google Bookmarks, you may be asked to log in again using your Google Account.)

Getting the most from Google Desktop Gadgets

After Google Desktop Gadgets are installed, you might find that your maximized browser window does not fully cover the screen. You can temporarily close the sidebar by clicking the Google Minimize button. When you minimize the sidebar, the Google search bar is displayed in the Windows taskbar.

Show a hidden Google sidebar by clicking the Restore button in the system tray, or by clicking Start on the taskbar, clicking All Programs (Vista), clicking Google Desktop, then clicking Google Desktop Sidebar. Select Always on Top from the Gadget menu to always have gadgets visible.

FIGURE A-14: iGoogle link

FIGURE A-15: Personalize iGoogle settings

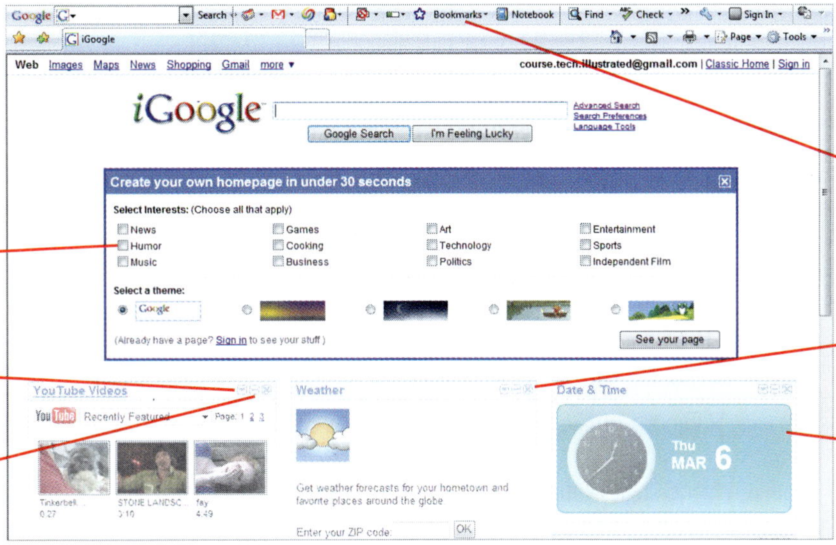

FIGURE A-16: Google Desktop Gadgets

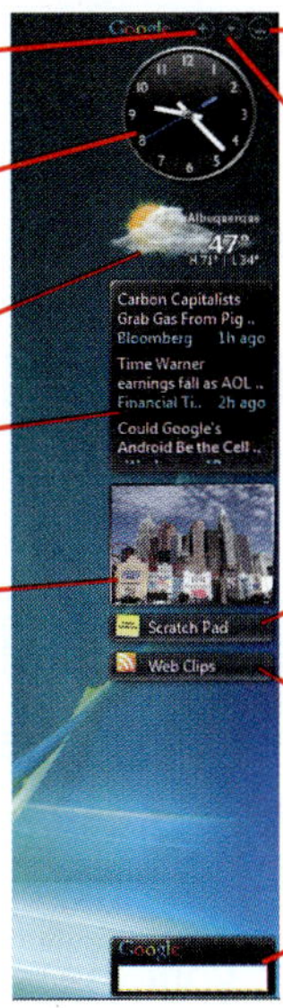

TABLE A-3: Some Google Desktop Gadgets

name	name	name
Art of the Day	Currency Converter	Technology News
Baseball News	Google Calendar	Temperature Converter
Best Flights Travel Search	Music Player	Ticket Finder
Best-Selling Books	Package Tracking	TicketsNow
Clock	Star Trek Trivia	Website monitor

UNIT
A
Google

Collecting Information with Google Notebook

The power of Google is enhanced by **Google Notebook**, a program that lets you collect and save text clippings, images, and links from Web pages all from within a browser window. Each notebook (and you can create as many as you want) can be divided into sections. You can use Google Notebook to organize your thoughts or create your own "action items" regardless of where you are or whose computer you're using. You can open Google Notebook by clicking more from the Google search screen menu, clicking even more, then clicking Notebook, or by pointing your browser to **notebook.google.com**, then logging in with your Google Account.

WHY IT'S IMPORTANT

- Just like a loose-leaf or spiral-bound notebook you might use to organize different academic subjects, Google Notebook can be used to organize your thoughts using drag-and-drop notes. Like many other Google products, Google Notebook is Web based and can be used from any computer with an Internet connection. Google Notebook is shown in Figure A-17.
- A Google Notebook can be shared with friends and colleagues by making your notebook public. You can open the mini Google Notebook pane from your browser window by clicking the Notebook button on the Google Toolbar. With Google Notebook, you'll never be caught without your work, and you won't need to carry an assortment of flash drives. Just log in to your Google Account, navigate to Google Notebook, and your work will be there. Figure A-18 shows the small-pane version of Google Notebook. From this pane, you can access all your notebooks, without having to open a new browser window. This means you can work more efficiently without having to open and close multiple browser windows. To find out more about Google Notebook, do a Google search on Google Notebook FAQ. The Google Notebook FAQ screen is shown in Figure A-19.
- Firefox users can point their browsers to **www.google.com/notebook/download** to download and install the Google Notebook Firefox Extension that will enable them to use the mini Google Notebook pane.

QUICK TIP

When the mini Google Notebook pane is open, you can select content from a Web page and drag it into your notebook.

USING GOOGLE NOTEBOOK: THE PERFECT ON-THE-ROAD TOOL

A good road warrior always makes sure he/she has all of the necessary equipment to get everything done. Using Google Notebook makes working from the road that much easier. By using Google products such as Search, Images, and Notebook, you will have all the resources you need to research and record your thoughts and observations.

1. **Log in to your Google Account, click the Notebook button in your browser's status bar, search for Google Notebook, or go to www.google.com/notebook**
2. **Click the Create a new notebook link, type Notes on Google Notebook, then click OK**
3. **When you're finished typing your ideas, click the Save now button**
4. **Point your browser to Google News at news.google.com, then click on a story of interest to you**
5. **Select text in a story, then drag the selection into the notebook you just created**

Turning Google Notebook data into a feed

If you can create a Google Notebook that can be viewed by others, why can't you turn that content into a feed? Well, you can. (A **feed** is a data source that can be periodically updated and then automatically accessed by others.) To find out more about turning your Google Notebook into a feed, point your browser to code.google.com/apis/notebook.

FIGURE A-17: Google Notebook

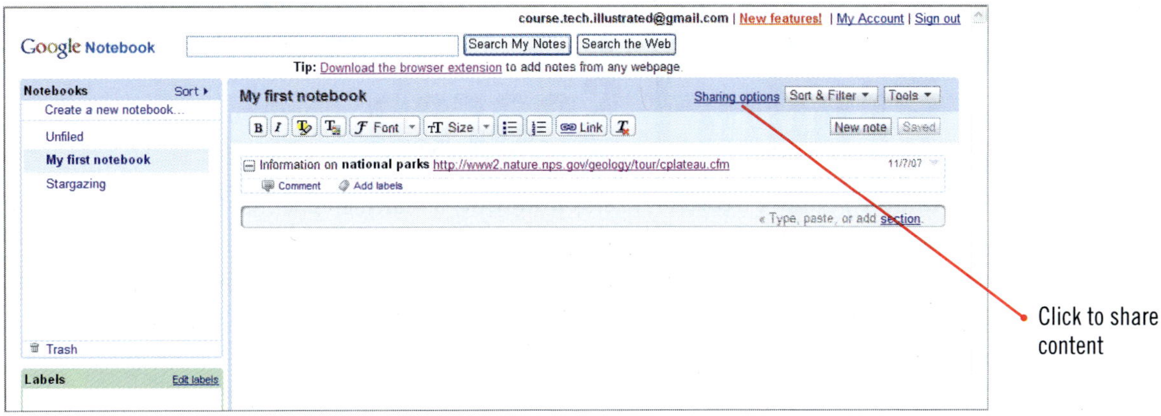

FIGURE A-18: Mini Google Notebook pane

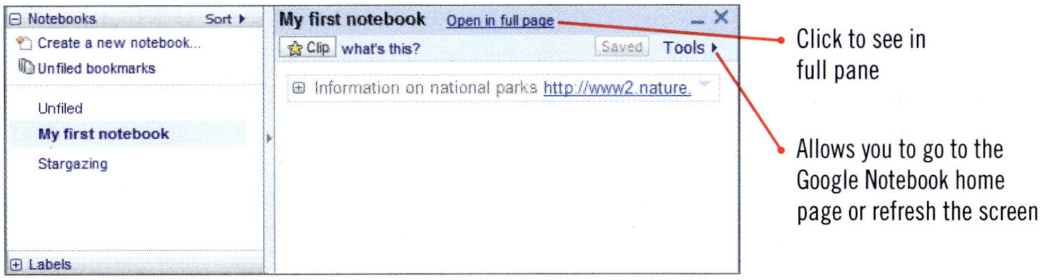

FIGURE A-19: Google Notebook features

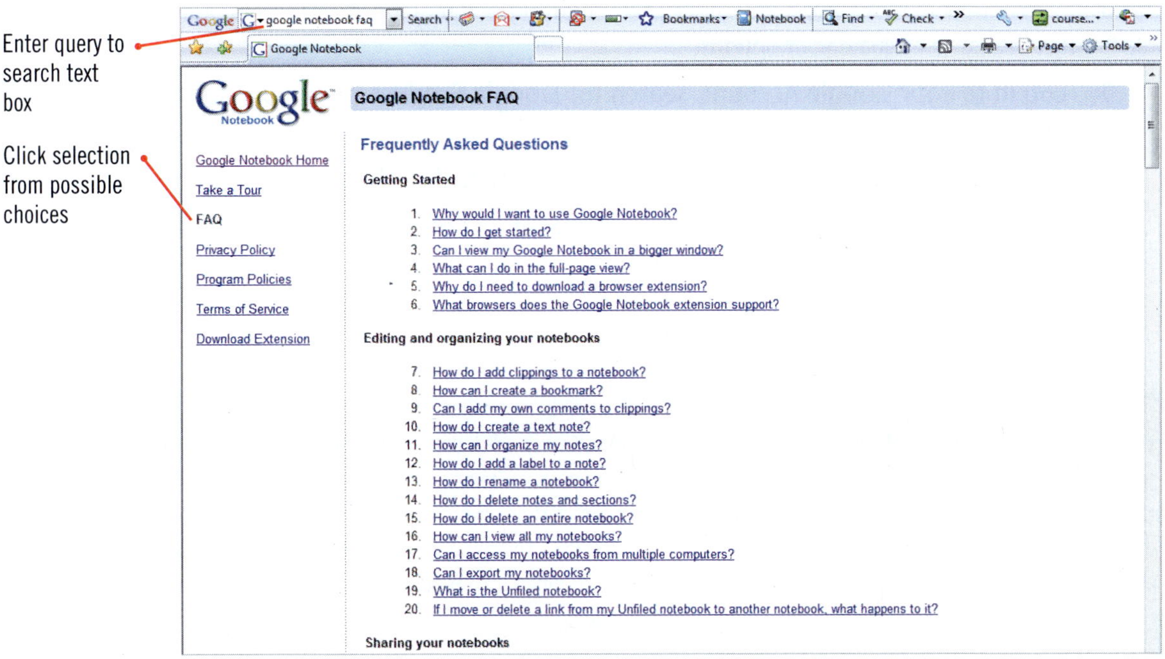

Google

Shopping with Google Product Search

Google Product Search is a **shopping bot**, a search engine that finds shopping deals at multiple shopping Web sites, listing both store name and price. Online shopping is wonderfully convenient, but hopping from one Web site to another can be inefficient and often annoying. With Google Product Search, you type in what you want and let Product Search do all the running around. **Google Catalogs** catalog search lets you browse and search merchant catalogs from the comfort of your computer. You can open Google Product Search by clicking Shopping from the Google search screen menu, or by pointing your browser to **www.google.com/products**.

WHY IT'S IMPORTANT

- **Google Product Search**
  Shopping takes time. The ultimate way to save time shopping is to do it from your desk. So why waste time looking at Web site after Web site when Google can do that for you? The Google Product Search Web site, shown in Figure A-20, looks a lot like the standard Google search site. But the results you get from the two sites are quite different. The displayed results of Google Product Search are items you can purchase (no informational sites are included), as shown in Figure A-21. When you're finished, you can easily check out by clicking the Google Checkout button. This feature lets you create multiple accounts and passwords and make purchases from multiple online stores. You might want multiple accounts so you don't confuse business and personal purchases. All your purchases can be tracked thorough a single source, with full fraud protection from Google.
- **Google Catalogs**
  Using the categories in Google Catalog, you can see a variety of merchant catalogs in a single location. Figure A-22 shows merchant catalogs in the Art Supplies category of Arts & Crafts. When you click on any of the catalog thumbnails, you'll see readable catalog pages that you can see in a Thumbnail View, 2-Page View, 1-Page View, or Enlarged View. The merchant's telephone number and Web site link are also provided.

SHOPPING FOR THE BEST PRICE

Imagine that you need to buy a new laptop computer. Rather than choosing several manufacturers' or store Web sites, you decide to use Google Product Search to evaluate your options.

1. **Log in to your Google Account, search for Google Product Search, or go to www.google.com/products**
2. **Type laptop computer in the Search text box, then click the Search Products button**
3. **Click the Show grid view link to see a different arrangement of the entries**

Making shopping a breeze with Google Shopping List

Did you notice that beneath each item in Google Product Search was a link to Add to Shopping List? The Google Shopping List is a feature you can access by pointing your browser to **www.google.com/shoppinglist**. It makes it possible for you to access items you selected from any computer. Using this feature, you can sort items by price, item, or date. As you peruse Google Product Search, click the Add to Shopping List link while in list view to capture those items of particular interest to you. (The Add to Shopping List link is not available in grid view.) You can even create a Wish List: a shopping list you can make public for those special occasions when it's important that your friends know exactly what you want.

FIGURE A-20: Google Product Search screen

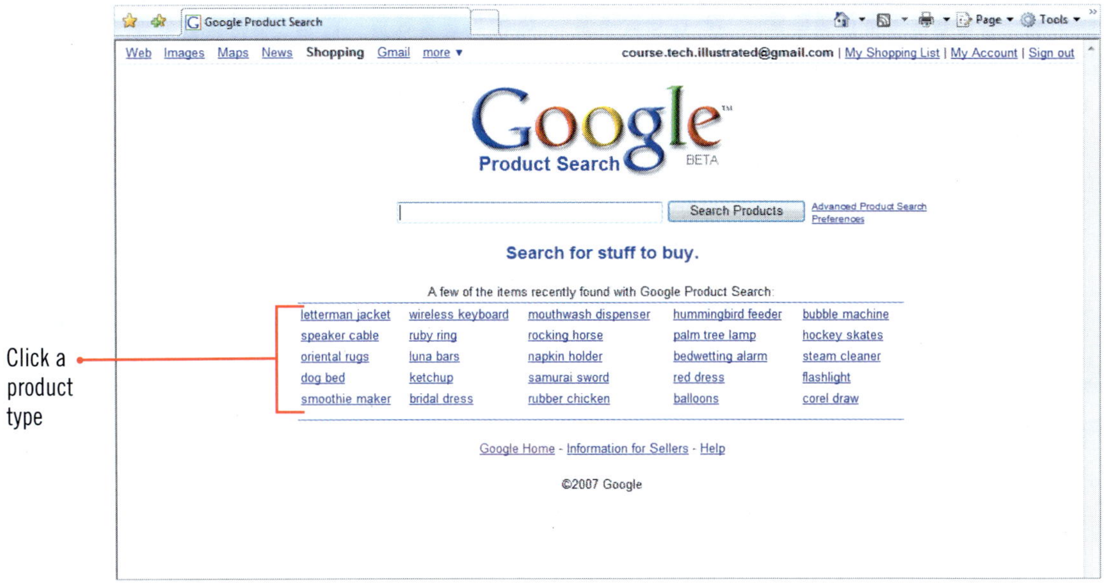

FIGURE A-21: Google Products results

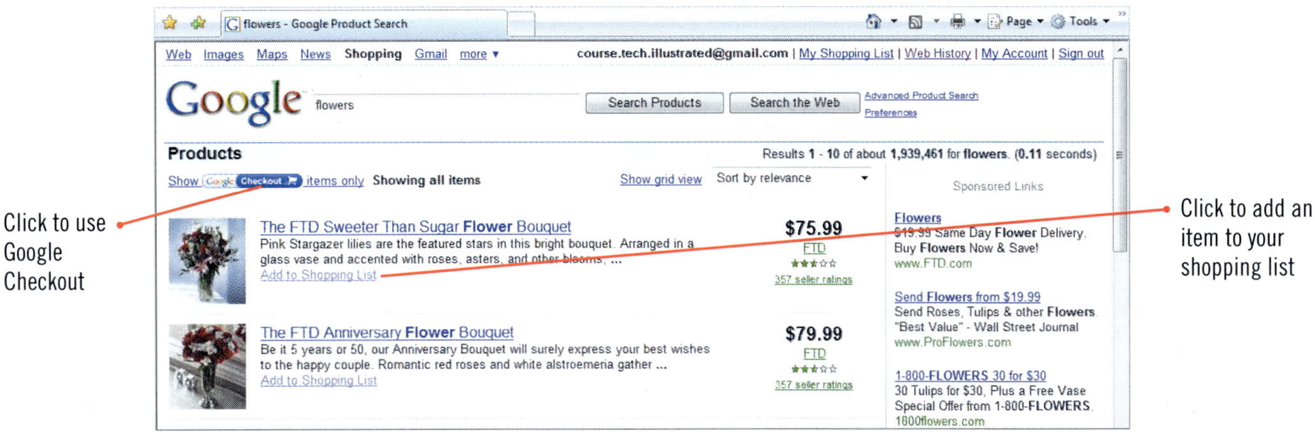

FIGURE A-22: Google Catalog Search screen

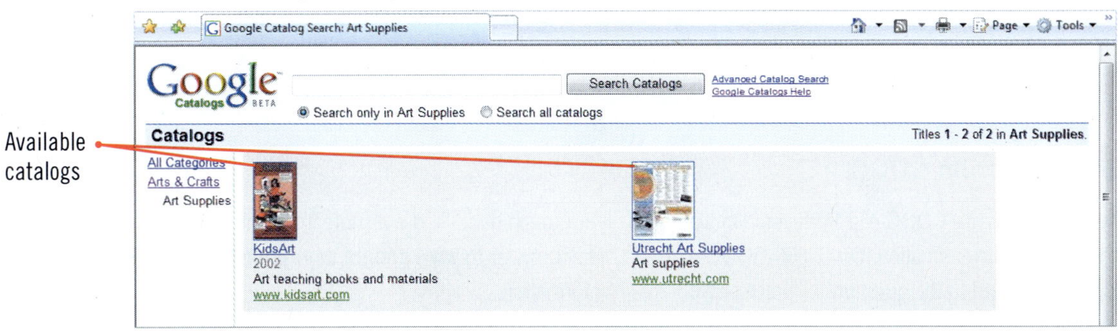

Google

UNIT A

Google

Finding Your Way Using Your Phone

You've already seen how you can use Google Maps to find directions, then send those directions to your cellular phone. But Google offers a number of tools and services you can access directly from your cellular phone, to help you stay connected and up to date while on the road or away from your computer. You can find all of Google's products for mobile devices by pointing your browser to **www.google.com/mobile**.

WHY IT'S IMPORTANT

QUICK TIP

Depending on your usage plan, using some features may result in additional charges.

- **Google Maps for Mobile**

  Using **Google Maps for Mobile**, available by clicking the Maps link and shown in Figure A-23, not only can you use Google maps and directions on your cell phone, but you also can get real-time traffic reports in over 30 major U.S. metropolitan areas. For more information identifying your location when using Google Maps for Mobile, click the Learn more link under the Where am I? heading. The interactive demo, shown in Figure A-24, is available through the Demo link and provides an overview of just how much this powerful program can do. (You might have to install Java on your computer to fully experience this page.)

- **Google Mobile**

  Google Mobile wireless service, shown in Figure A-25, lets you use many Google products on your mobile device. When you click the Get started now button, you will be prompted to enter your cell phone number. Google will then send your phone a text message that includes a link that you can use on your cell phone browser to access Google Mobile products. Google products that you can access from your mobile device include Google search, Gmail, Picasa, YouTube, and GOOG-411, among others. GOOG-411 helps you to find the business or phone number you are looking for by voice, instead of typing on your cell phone's number pad.

- **Google SMS**

  You can text Google from your cell phone for information such as weather, movie times, and sports scores using Google SMS (Short Message Service), the Google text message service.

SENDING INFORMATION TO YOUR MOBILE PHONE

If you find yourself always on the go from city to city and hotel to hotel, you can take full advantage of all that Google Mobile has to offer. Use Google Mobile to keep you knowledgeable about where you are headed. If your mobile device does not have these capabilities, review these steps instead of performing them:

1. **Open your browser and log in to your Google Account**
2. **Point your browser to www.google.com/mobile**
3. **Click the Get started now button, enter the phone number of your mobile device (entering the area code and number), then click Send now**
4. **Follow the instructions in the text message sent from Google Mobile, then click the SMS link**
5. **Open a new text message, type weather Boston, then send it to Google at 466453**

Getting information from GOOG-411

You can use the free Google service GOOG-411 from your landline or cell phone to find local business information. Dial 1-800-GOOG-411 (1-800-466-4411), then respond to the questions by voice or with your touch pad. Find out more information by pointing your browser to **www.google.com/goog411** to find out more information.

FIGURE A-23: Google Maps for Mobile

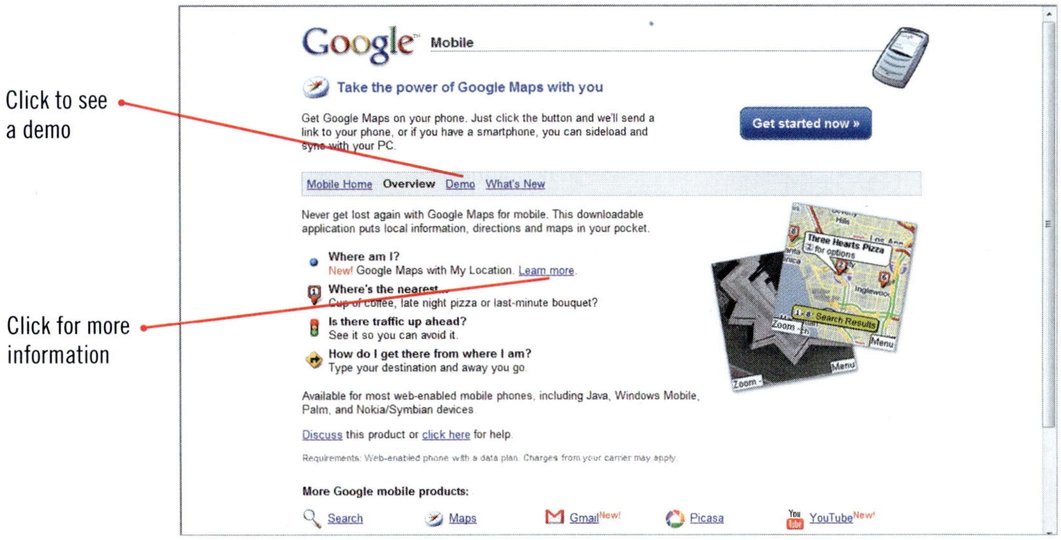

FIGURE A-24: Google Maps for Mobile demo

FIGURE A-25: Google Mobile

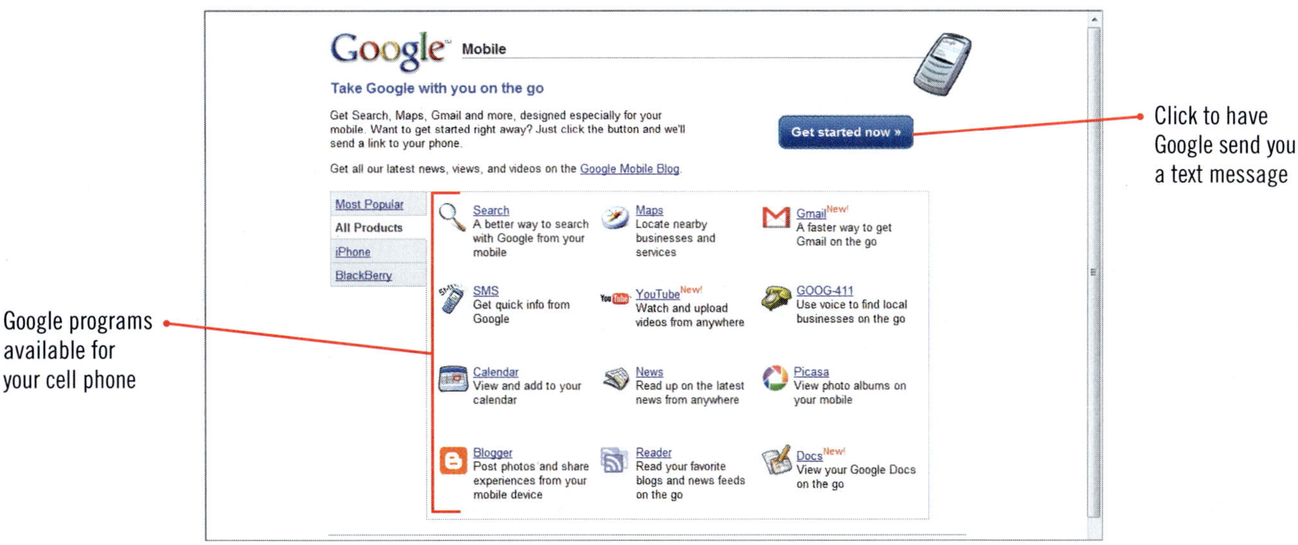

UNIT A
Google

Using Google Help

Many of the individual Google programs have their own specific Help pages, with answers to frequently asked questions (FAQs), but if you need additional assistance, you can always find it by visiting the **Google Help** page. You can open Google Help by pointing your browser to **www.google.com/support**.

WHY IT'S IMPORTANT

- Even an intuitive group of programs needs to provide support to their users. Google has a large array of products, so it would be impossible for anyone to know everything about how each one works. When you look at the list of all Google products, shown in Figure A-26, you can see just how many there are. To find out more information about any of the services in this list, click its link. Google products are organized by category, and you can review a list of products in alphabetical order at **www.google.com/options**.
- Google also offers Google Help Groups, which are communities of other users who can help you get the most out of Google products. You can access these Help Groups by clicking the Learn from other Google users link on the main Google Help page, then clicking the link for the relevant product.
- Because Google updates its programs and offerings often, additions may make using Help a necessity.

GETTING HELP WHEN YOU NEED IT

Google services are incredibly rich and vast, so it's important that you know how to get help when you need it. You can access the Google Help system by typing **www.google.com/support** or use Google to search for Google Help. See Figure A-27. For information on specific Google products, click the official list of products link. Each of the links on this page takes you to the home page for a specific product, and many of these have their own Help links.

1. **Open your browser and point to** www.google.com/support
2. **Click the link for** Sketchup
3. **Click the link for** Using Sketchup with Google Earth
4. **Click the link** How do I place a Sketchup model in Google Earth
5. **Close the Help window when you're finished reading**

Using Google to get the most from your PC

By pointing your browser to **pack.google.com**, you can download free productivity software such as Norton Security Scan, Google Earth, Google Desktop, Firefox, Picasa, RealPlayer, Google Photos Screensaver, Google Talk, StarOffice, Spyware Doctor, Adobe Reader, and Skype. These programs are not trial versions or spyware and you can download any or all of them whenever you want. This list changes frequently, so check back often for new offerings. Help with programs in the Google Pack is available by clicking the Pack Help Group link or by pointing your browser to **groups.google.com/group/google-pack**.

FIGURE A-26: More Google Products

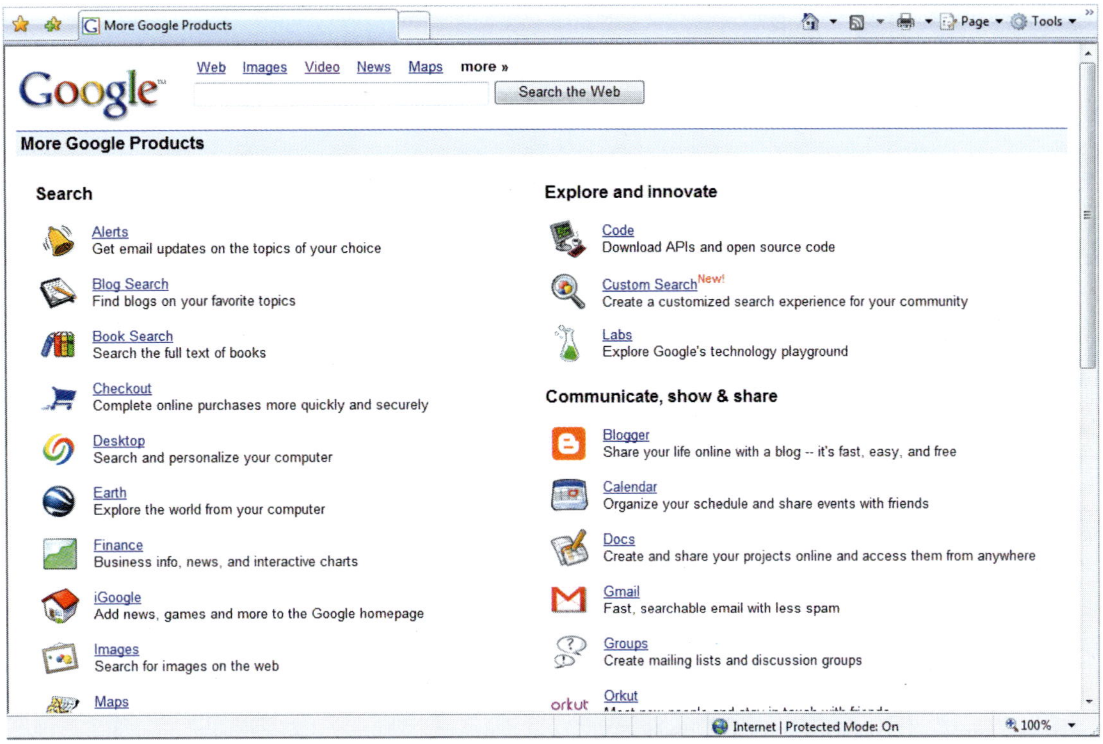

FIGURE A-27: Google Help

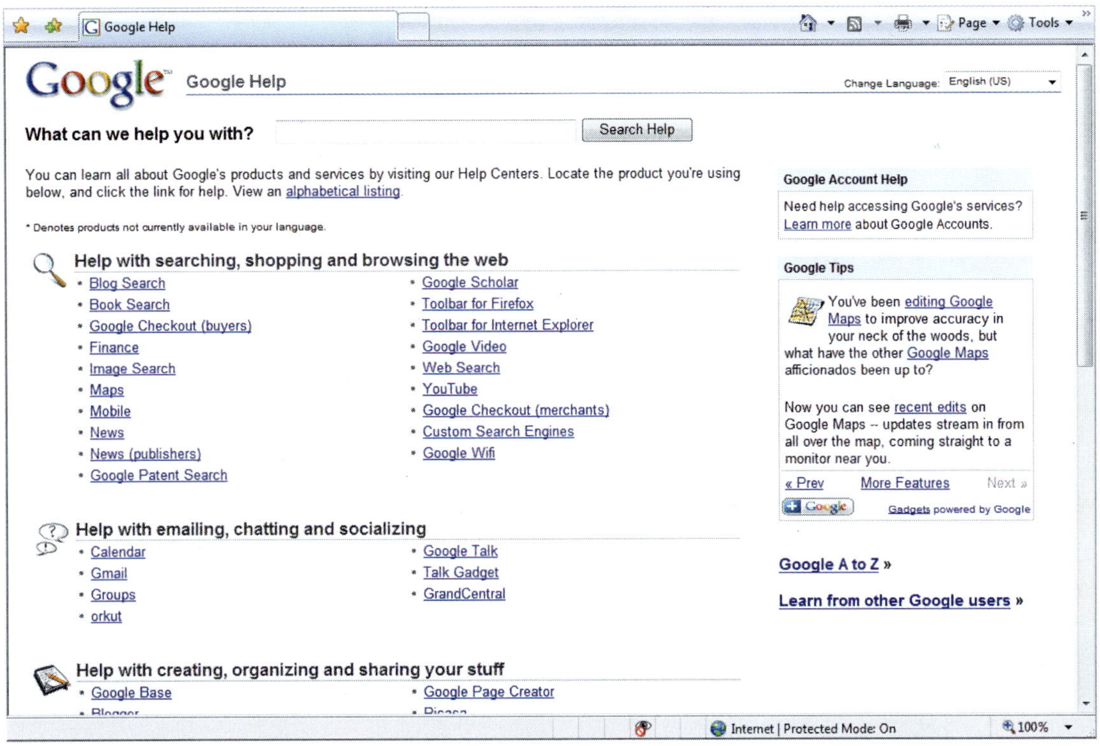

Practice

If you have a SAM user profile, you may have access to hands-on instruction, practice, and assessment of the skills covered in this unit. Log in to your SAM account (http://sam2007.course.com/) to launch any assigned training activities or exams that relate to the skills covered in this unit.

▼ CONCEPTS REVIEW

Label the elements of Google Toolbar and iGoogle shown in Figure A-28.

FIGURE A-28

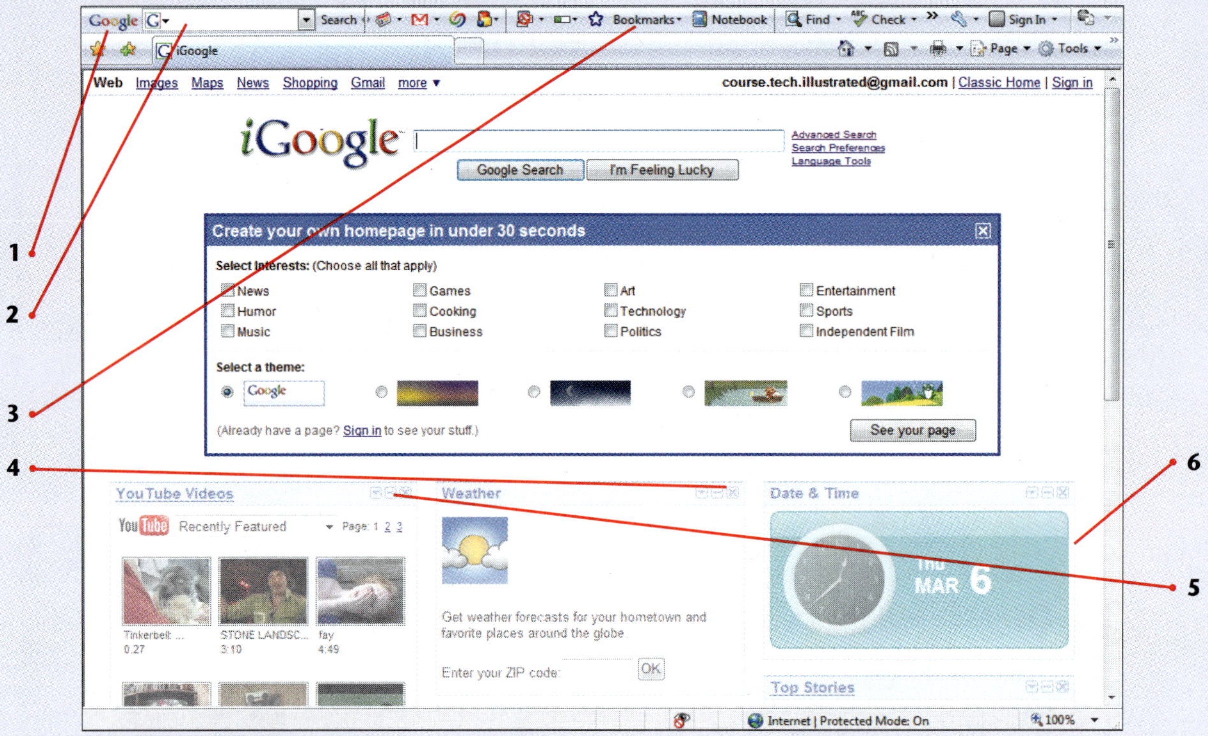

Match each Google program with the statement that best describes it.

7. Mobile	**a.** Finds images on the Web
8. Alerts	**b.** Lets you use Google programs on your cell phone
9. Maps	**c.** Contains a search box from which you can make Google searches
10. Toolbar	**d.** Lets you search and browse merchant catalogs
11. Images	**e.** E-mails updates on specific topics
12. Catalogs	**f.** Lets you view maps and get directions on your computer

Select the best answer from the list of choices.

13. You can perform a Google search from which of the following:
- **a.** The Google Toolbar and any browser page
- **b.** The Google search text box gadget (if installed)
- **c.** *www.google.com*
- **d.** All of the above

14. Which Google program is used to personalize your desktop?
- **a.** Products
- **b.** Desktop
- **c.** iGoogle
- **d.** Notebook

15. Which of the following statements is true about the Google Toolbar?
- **a.** It is installed separately on your computer.
- **b.** You can use any search engine from it.
- **c.** It shows you suggestions as you type search criteria.
- **d.** A and C

16. Which feature lets you see what Web sites you have visited?
- **a.** History Finder
- **b.** Web History
- **c.** Bookmarker
- **d.** Retracer

17. Which Google program gives you directions to a specific location?
- **a.** Google Find it
- **b.** Google Images
- **c.** Google Maps
- **d.** Google Driver

18. Which Google program will send directions to your cellular phone?
- **a.** Google Video
- **b.** Google iMap
- **c.** Google Phone
- **d.** Google Maps

19. What is the name of Google programs installed on your desktop?
- **a.** Widgets
- **b.** Gimmicks
- **c.** Geegaws
- **d.** Gadgets

20. Which Google program is used to create a personalized home page?
- **a.** eGoogle
- **b.** Google Desktop
- **c.** iGoogle
- **d.** Google Mobile

21. Which of the following Google features *does not* require installation on your computer?
- **a.** Google Earth
- **b.** Google Bookmarks
- **c.** Google Desktop
- **d.** Google Toolbar

22. Which statement is true about Google Notebook?
- **a.** It requires installation, but no Internet connection.
- **b.** It lets you organize your thoughts and is Web based.
- **c.** It lets you store your work on thumb drives.
- **d.** It is part of the Google Desktop program.

23. Which Google program is a shopping bot?
- **a.** Google Catalogs
- **b.** Google Product Search
- **c.** Google Notebook
- **d.** Google Gadgets

24. Use ______________ to use Google programs on your mobile device.
- **a.** Google Maps
- **b.** Google Cell Phone
- **c.** Google Maps for Mobile
- **d.** Google Mobile

▼ INDEPENDENT CHALLENGE 1

You are planning a business trip to Washington, D.C. While there, you want to play tourist and see certain national landmarks. You plan to use a Google Gadget (such as Best Flights Travel Search Gadget) to find a flight and hotel, and use Google Maps to help you get from your hotel to the White House at 1600 Pennsylvania Avenue, NW.

- **a.** Open your browser and log in to your Google Account, if necessary.
- **b.** Point your browser to the Google search screen, or use your Google Toolbar to find out the days and hours when the White House is open for tours.
- **c.** Install a gadget, such as the one shown in Figure A-29, that lets you find flights to Washington, D.C., then find a well-priced flight and hotel for a four-day stay in the nation's capital.
- **d.** Locate at least one restaurant near your hotel and send directions to your cell phone.
- **e.** Open Google Maps, and enter the Start address (your hotel).
- **f.** Enter the End address (the White House).
- **g.** Get the directions.
- **h.** Print the page, then exit Google Maps.

FIGURE A-29

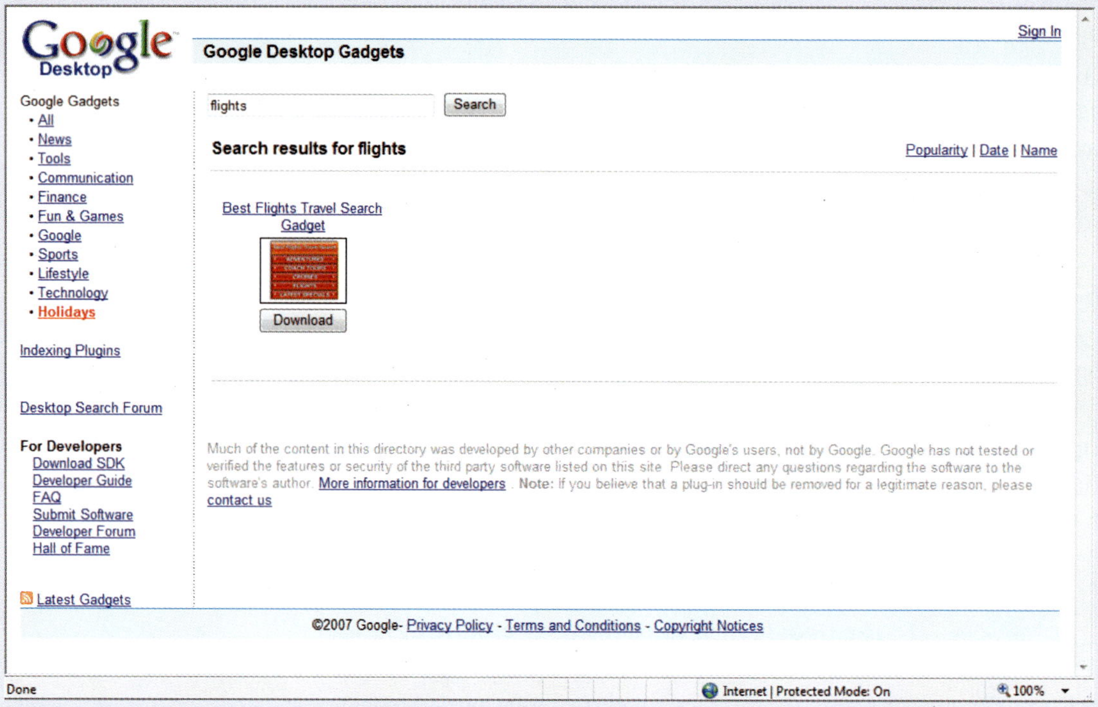

▼ INDEPENDENT CHALLENGE 2

Your position as IT manager at a start-up company means you need to get up to speed on digital devices and how they can be used. You've decided to give yourself a crash course in these devices using the many available Google programs.

- **a.** Open your browser and go to the Google search page.
- **b.** Acquaint yourself with the variety of digital devices by searching Google Images, then print the page and compare your results with Figure A-30. Which digital devices pictured do you have?
- **c.** Use Google Notebook to capture and record your data.
- **d.** Use Google Products to compare prices of various digital devices and record your results in Google Notebook.
- **e.** Use Google Bookmarks to record the sites you visit that have the best prices.
- **f.** Review the programs offered by Google Mobile and explore whether any are designed specifically for use with the Blackberry mobile device.

FIGURE A-30

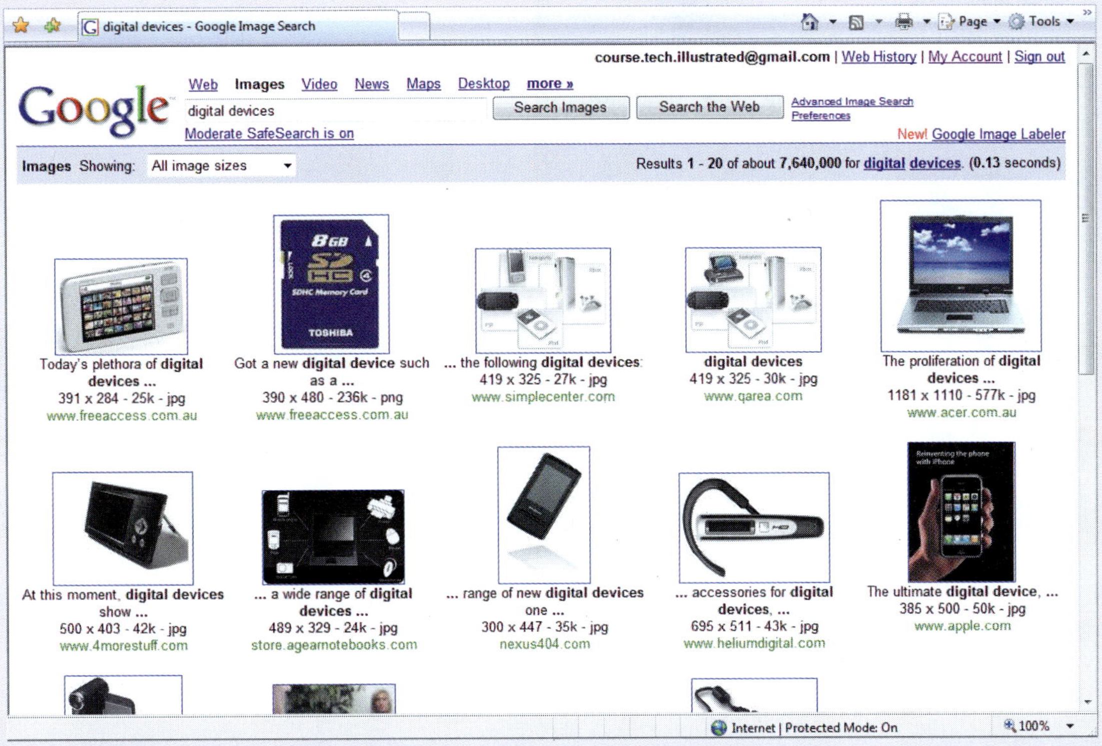

▼ VISUAL WORKSHOP

Use Google Earth to locate the White House using the skills you learned in this unit. Click the link for the White House, compare your image with Figure A-31, then print the page.

FIGURE A-31

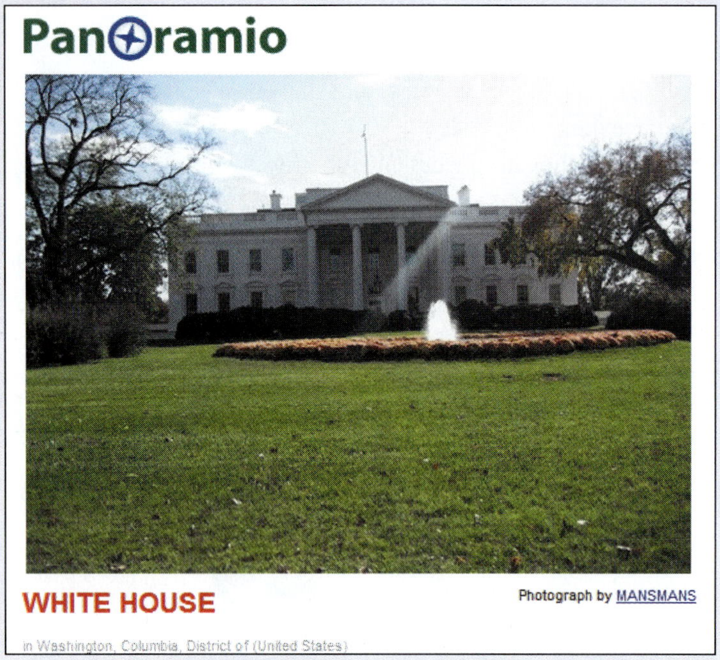

UNIT B Google

Expanding Your Productivity

Now that you have learned some of the basic programs and services available from Google, you will learn how to use features that will make you more productive. Google provides an amazing arsenal of communication tools with which you can create, receive, and send e-mail messages, make appointments, share images, manage subscriptions, and communicate instantly.

OBJECTIVES

- Communicate with Gmail
- Chat instantly with Google Talk
- Create and use Google Groups
- Blog with Google
- Enhance your blog
- Make appointments with Google Calendar
- Track financial assets
- Use Google Docs
- Manage images with Picasa

UNIT
B
Google

Communicating with Gmail

The Google e-mail program, called **Gmail**, is a Web-based e-mail client. This means that you can use it from any computer with an Internet connection. With Gmail, you can create, receive, reply, and archive communications with other Internet users. Gmail can be opened by clicking Gmail on the Google menu bar or by pointing your browser to **mail.google.com**.

WHY IT'S IMPORTANT

QUICK TIP
Messages are displayed in chronological order, with the newest message at the top of the list. Click Reply to respond to an existing message; click Forward to send a message to someone else.

- ### Create and reply to e-mail messages
  Using your Gmail account, you can keep in touch with other Internet users. After the Gmail screen is displayed, as shown in Figure B-1, you can read and reply to messages. The left side of the screen contains areas that allow you access to many advanced operations, such as creating labels, chatting, and inviting others to use Gmail. You can expand and collapse these areas by clicking the triangle found at the left of the area name.
  - The Add Cc link is used to send a "carbon copy" to another recipient, which is useful for including someone on an e-mail message who is not directly involved with the subject matter, but might be interested in the content. Recipients who have been carbon copied are visible to all the recipients of the e-mail message.
  - The Add Bcc link is used to send a "blind carbon copy" to a recipient. Recipients who have been blind carbon copied on an e-mail message are invisible to all of the other recipients. This is useful for including on an e-mail message someone whose receipt of the message does not need to be known by all the recipients.

- ### Stay connected
  While you are working on your computer, you can leave Gmail open in your browser. You can see if there are any new messages by clicking the Refresh link. A message can be deleted (whether it's been read or not) by clicking the check box to the left of the star, then clicking the Delete button. You can create a new message by clicking the Compose Mail link. You type the text of a message in the large box at the bottom of the screen, as shown in Figure B-2.

QUICK TIP
Contact names matching your keystrokes are displayed as you type in the To text box of an e-mail message.

- ### Keep track of contacts
  Use the Contacts list to record important information, such as name, address, phone numbers, and e-mail addresses, of those with whom you correspond. Click the Edit button, shown in Figure B-3, to add information to each contact. You can add a picture to any contact by clicking the Add a picture link that is displayed after the initial contact information has been entered. You can use most graphic images (in formats such as .jpg, .gif, and .png) already on your computer.

QUICK TIP
Labels can be created either before or after messages are received.

- ### Organize messages
  You can organize your messages using the Labels feature to create categories just as you would with file folders. Although it's not necessary to do so, labeling your e-mail can make sifting through all your messages much easier. To create labels for your messages, click the Edit labels link, type a label in the Create a new label text box, then click Create. To delete a label, click the Edit labels link, click the remove link to the right of the label name, then click OK.

SENDING E-MAIL

You and your teammates are getting ready to prepare your sections of the annual report. You are each working independently, but want feedback from each other. You will use Gmail to communicate with one another.

1. **Open Gmail and sign in to your Google Account, if necessary**
2. **Enter contact information for your instructor and at least two classmates**
3. **Click the Compose Mail link, then include both classmates in the To list**
4. **Add your instructor's e-mail address using the Add Cc link**
5. **Attach an existing document to the message**
6. **Send the message**

FIGURE B-1: Gmail inbox

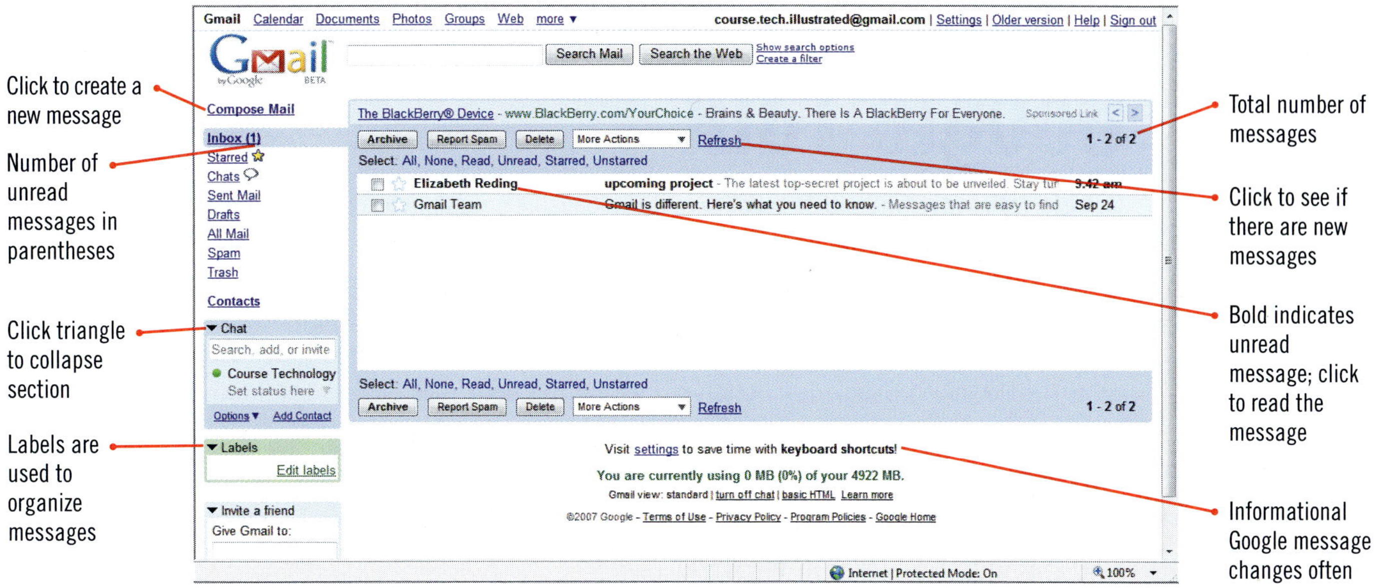

FIGURE B-2: Composing a message

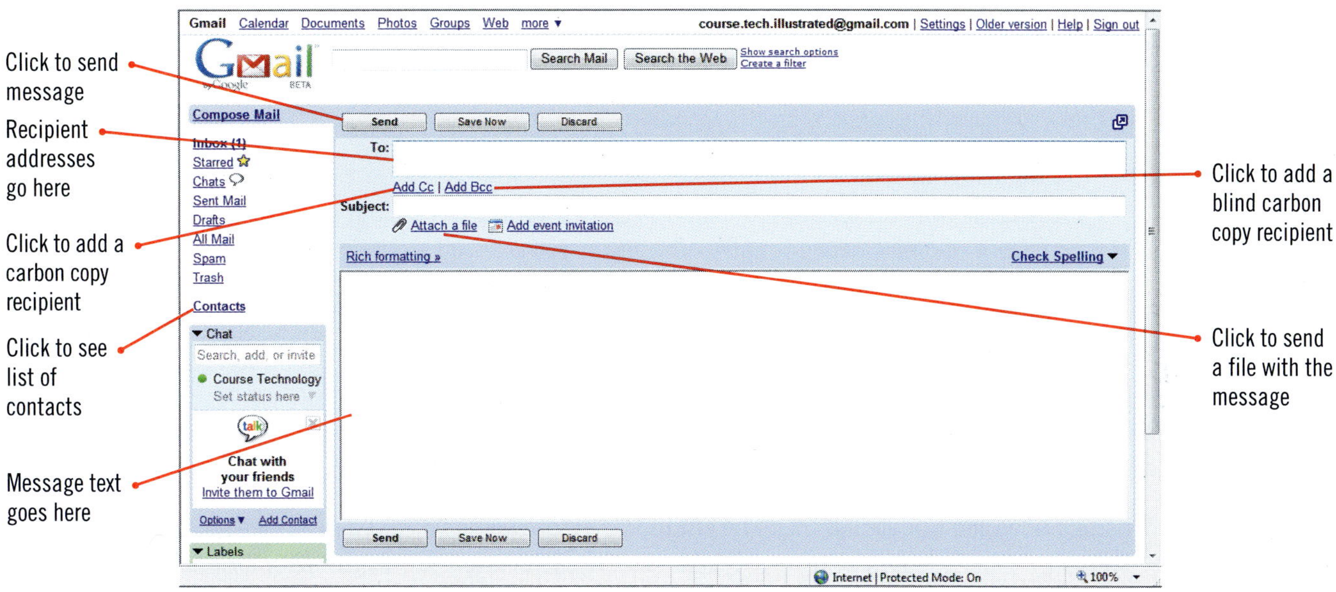

FIGURE B-3: Gmail Contacts

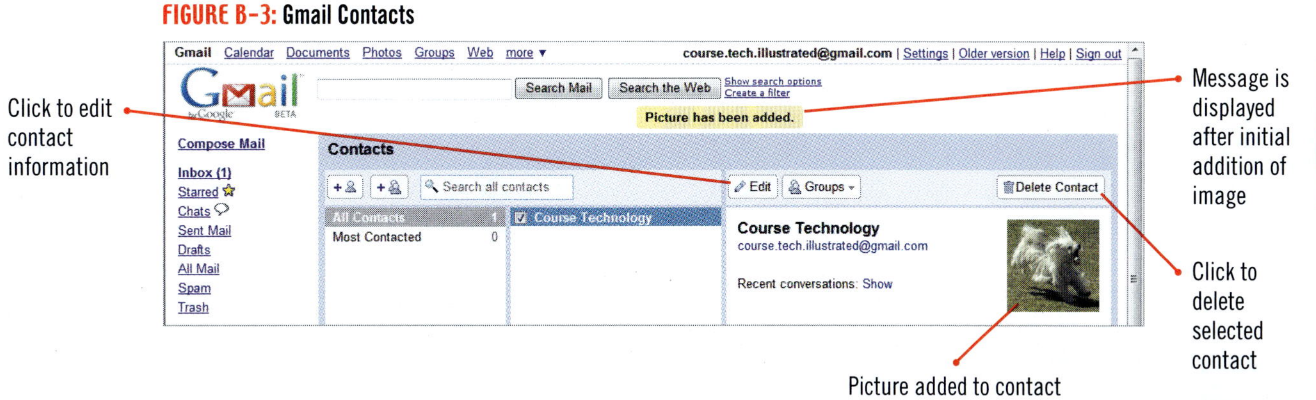

Google

UNIT B
Google

Chatting Instantly with Google Talk

Google Talk instant messaging service is a downloadable program you can use to chat instantly with others using instant messaging, Gmail notifications, PC-to-PC voice calls, and file transfers. If you prefer, you can use Google Talk on the Web with the Google Talk Gadget without having to install any additional software on your computer. If you don't have the Google Talk Gadget or if Google Talk is not installed on your computer, you can get it by pointing your browser to **www.google.com/talk**, then clicking either the Download Google Talk button or the Launch Google Talk Gadget link shown in Figure B-4. You can also access Google Talk from within Gmail.

WHY IT'S IMPORTANT

QUICK TIP

You can sign out of Google Talk or the Google Talk Gadget by clicking the status list arrow, then clicking Sign out (Google Talk) or Sign out of chat (Google Talk Gadget).

- **Chat instantly with other users**

  After you have installed Google Talk on your computer or have opened the Google Talk Gadget, the names of your Google contacts are displayed in the contacts area. When you place your mouse pointer over an available contact in Google Talk, the Chat window shown in Figure B-5 is displayed. You can click the Chat, Send voicemail, or Call buttons to initiate a Google Talk session. Figure B-6 shows an online chat session. Figure B-7 shows the other side of the same chat session using the Google Talk Gadget. For more information on Google Talk and the Google Talk Gadget, click the About Google Talk link.

QUICK TIP

You can also use Google Talk to send files to another user. Click the Send Files button, locate and select the file on your computer, then click Send.

- **Call another user**

  You can call another user using a voice mail message or an actual call through your computer. When you call someone who isn't around to answer the phone, you can send a voice mail message. This message is automatically sent as an attachment (as an MP3 file) to the other user's e-mail address. You will hear a prompt to leave a message, which is sent as an e-mail attachment that can then be played with any audio player. Users can use the Call feature only if both have installed Google Talk and a Gmail account.

TALKING THROUGH YOUR COMPUTER

Your phone bills are getting huge and Google Talk might be just the ticket to lower them. You'd like to see how this feature works and if it's practical to use on a frequent basis.

1. **Point your browser to www.google.com/talk and install Google Talk on your computer or click the Launch Google Talk Gadget link and log in with your Google Account, if necessary**
2. **Add the Google addresses of at least two other users**
3. **Contact one of the users in your Google Talk list and have a conversation**

Using Google Talk with other Google products

Once you have installed Google Talk and the Google Talk Gadget, you will be able to use a host of other Google products. For example, notifications of Gmail messages will appear in real-time (as they happen) in Google Talk. Your Gmail contacts are automatically displayed in Google Talk and you can chat with groups of users simultaneously. You can cut and paste video and slideshows from YouTube, Google Video video search, Picasa, and Flickr (a photo sharing program at **www.flickr.com**) into your chat windows for instant viewing. Google Talk is integrated into Gmail, so you can chat directly with any Gmail user. if you need to access a chat session, all Google Talk sessions (via a Gmail account) are saved to a searchable archive within Gmail.

FIGURE B-4: Google Talk page

FIGURE B-5: Google Talk Chat window

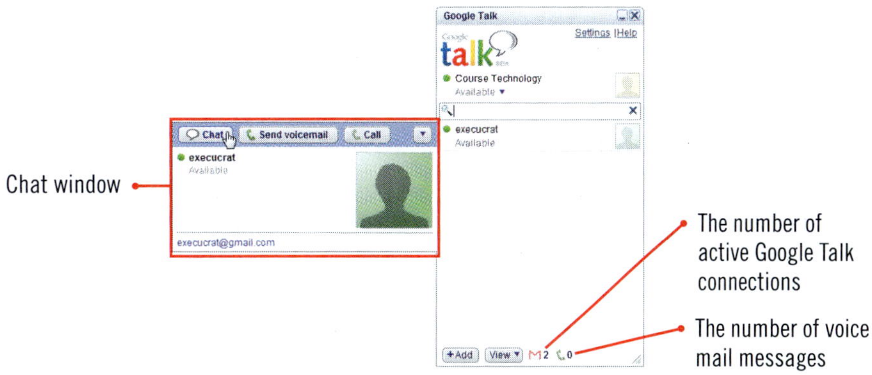

FIGURE B-6: Google Talk chat session

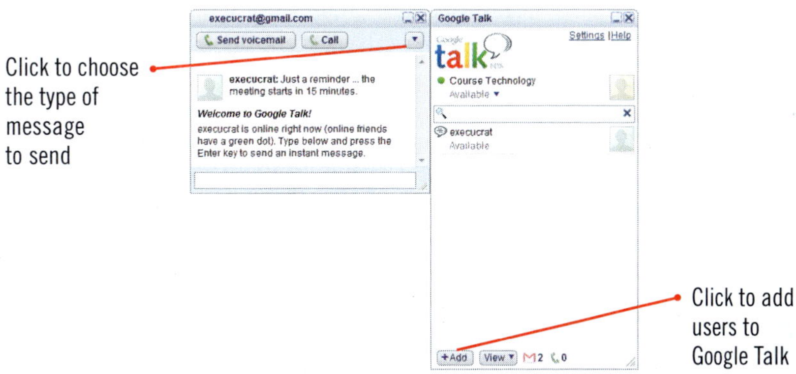

FIGURE B-7: Google Talk Gadget chat session

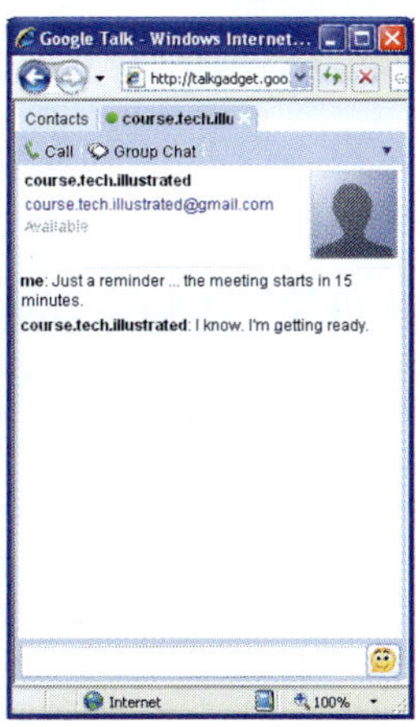

UNIT
B
Google

Creating and Using Google Groups

Google Groups discussion forums are a collection of public online forums in which you can participate. You can use Google Groups to join an existing group or start your own group, either online or by using e-mail, create custom pages, and utilize the knowledge of members to create a knowledge base. By joining a group, you can take advantage of the established knowledge and experiences of others, through e-mail as well as sharing files and contributing to knowledge databases. Using Google Groups, you can find out about LASIK surgery and the positive and negative experiences of other patients, exchange recipes, or join a grief support group. You can open Google Groups by clicking Groups from the Gmail, Calendar, Documents menu, or by pointing your browser to **groups.google.com**.

WHY IT'S IMPORTANT

- **Find an existing group**
  Using Google Groups, you can stay in touch with people who have similar interests. When you open Google Groups, you'll see the screen shown in Figure B-8. From this screen, you can explore what Google Groups has to offer by clicking the Take the tour link. See Figure B-9. The tour explains how you can use Google Groups. If you already know the name of a specific group, you can go to it by entering its name in the Find out what people are doing with Google Groups text box. You can also click one of the displayed groups, or see all the group categories by clicking the Browse all group categories link at the bottom of the screen. The Group directory, accessible by using the Browse all group categories link, lists all the available topics and the number of groups within each topic. The Group directory is shown in Figure B-10. In addition to being organized by topic, the directory also lists groups by region, language, activity, and membership. This means that if you want to join a Spanish-speaking group, for example, you can see what groups are available by clicking the Spanish link in the Language category.
- **Start your own group**
  If you can't find a group that matches your interests, you can start one of your own. When you click the Create a group link, you'll be able to select a name for your group and you'll create an e-mail address for contributors to your group. You can also decide whether anyone can access this group or if access is to be restricted to specific individuals.

JOINING A GROUP

You are interested in finding a group that discusses using computers.

1. **Open Google Groups and log in using your Google Account, if necessary**
2. **Click the Take the tour link to discover what Google Groups has to offer**
3. **Return to the initial Google Groups page, then click the Browse all group categories link**
4. **Click the People link in the Groups directory**
5. **Click the Computers link in the People category**
6. **Click the link of a topic in this category that you find interesting and join the group**

FIGURE B-8: What can you do with groups?

FIGURE B-9: Google Groups tour

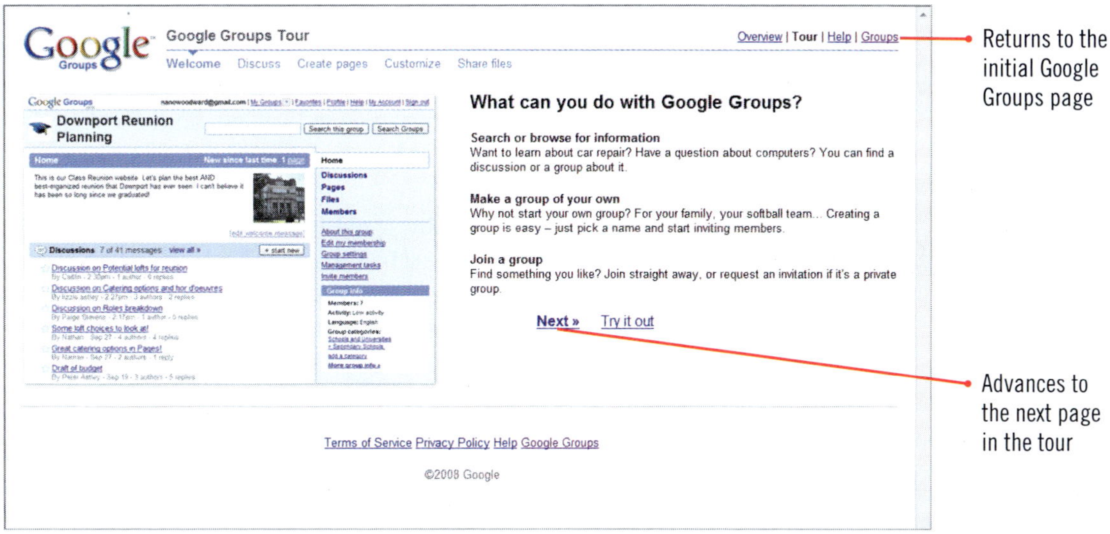

FIGURE B-10: Group directory

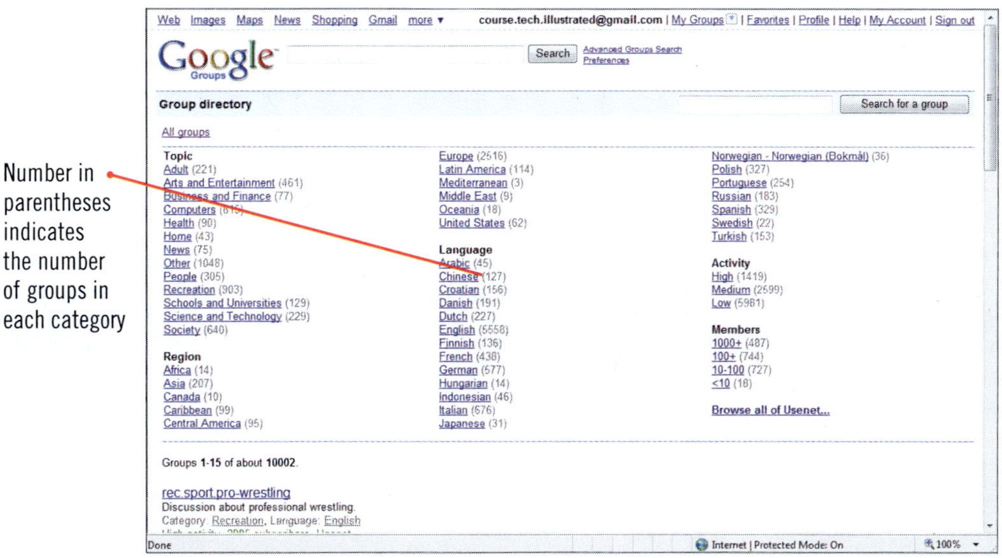

UNIT B
Google

Blogging with Google

Blogger Web publishing service is an online service that lets you create and maintain your own blogs (online journals), as well as read the contributions of other bloggers. Using a blog is a great way to share your thoughts with others and get their reactions. Using Blogger, you can record accounts of your personal experiences, keep in touch with family and friends, and express your political opinions. Blogger makes it easy to set up your own professional-looking blog, complete with colors and graphics. You can open Blogger by clicking More from the Google search screen menu, clicking Blogs, clicking More from the Google Blog Search menu, then clicking Blogger, or by pointing your browser to **www.blogger.com**, then logging in with your Google Account.

WHY IT'S IMPORTANT

QUICK TIP

No need to periodically save your work—Blogger saves your drafts automatically.

- **Create your own blog**

  Blogging can be great fun, and the process of making it look nice is fun too. When you open Blogger (but before you've logged in), you'll see the screen shown in Figure B-11. After you've created one or more of your own blogs, they'll be displayed in the Dashboard area. You can look at your existing blogs by clicking the View Blog link. Beneath the Dashboard are links for recent blogs that may be of interest. To set up your own blog, click the Create your blog now button or the Create a Blog link. The next step is to name your blog. Give your blog a meaningful title and blog address that you can give to others so they can directly access your blog. The next step is to choose a template for your blog. There are a dozen templates from which you can choose. Each template contains colors, fonts, and formatting so that you can concentrate on creating a compelling blog, rather than spending your time choosing fonts and formatting columns. Because only a small sample of each template is shown, you can use the preview template link under each sample to see a better view of how your blog will look. When you have found the template you want to use, select it, then click Continue. See Figure B-12. You'll see a notification telling you that your blog has been created. To add posts to your blog, or further customize it with different colors or fonts, click the Start posting link. When making posts to your blog, you'll see icons similar to those found in Gmail and other word processors, as shown in Figure B-13. When you're finished writing, click the Publish Post link.

- **Read the blogs of others**

  You can view video blogs using YouTube, and can see more blogger news by clicking the Blogger Buzz blog link at the bottom of the Blogger home page. Some companies use corporate blogs as a means of keeping the public informed of product developments. Many artists use blogs to keep in touch with those who appreciate their efforts.

- **Search for blogs**

  You can search for a specific blog without logging in to Blogger by pointing your browser to *blogsearch.google.com*, typing a topic or specific name in the Search text box, then clicking Search Blogs.

CREATING A BLOG

You wish your family were more connected. Rather than settle for the traditional end-of-year letter of accomplishments, you've decided to create a family blog.

1. **Point your browser to www.blogger.com and log in with your Google Account, if necessary**
2. **Create a blog called Your Surname Family Blog using a template you feel is appropriate**
3. **Send an e-mail containing the blog address to your family members and invite them to participate in the blog**
4. **Create an initial post and watch what happens**

FIGURE B-11: Google Blogger

FIGURE B-12: Blogger templates

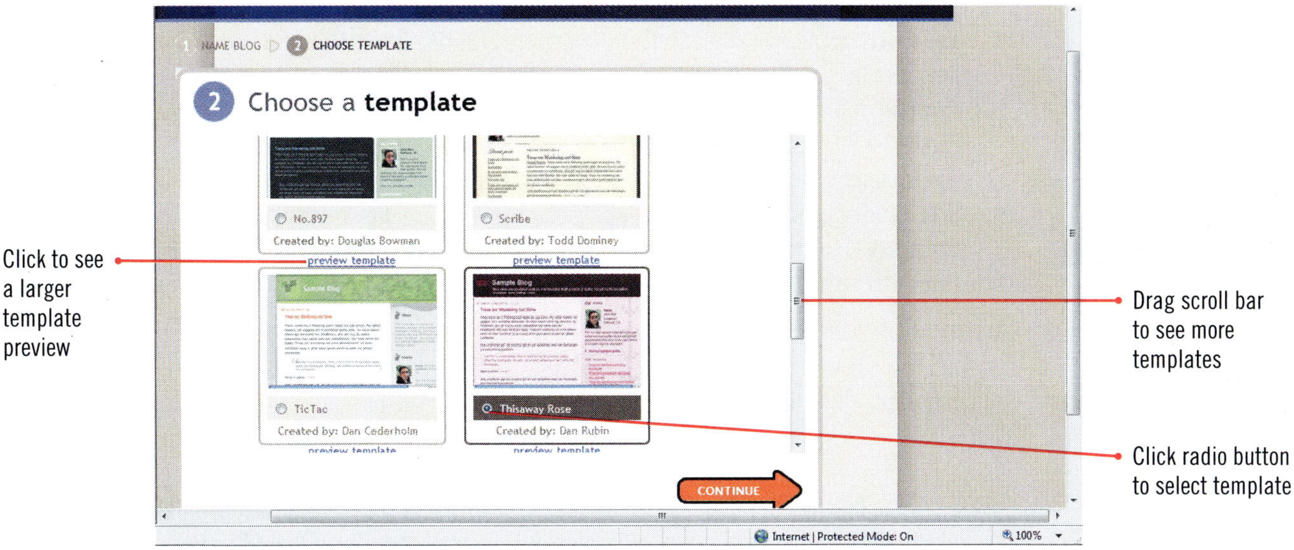

FIGURE B-13: Composing blog text

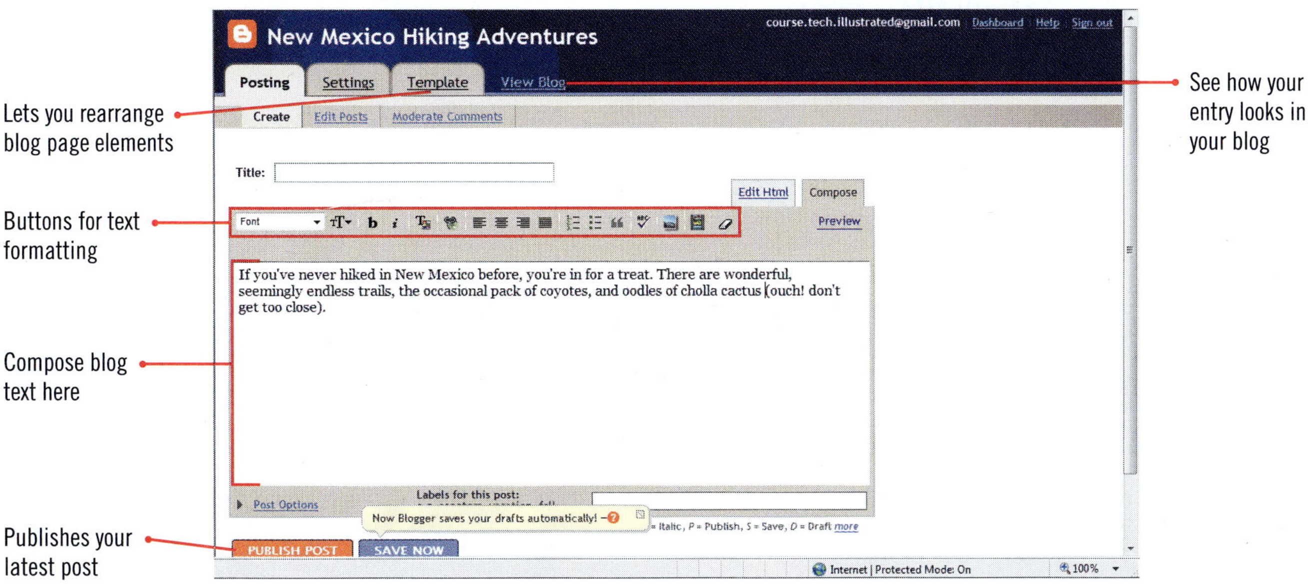

Google

Enhancing Your Blog

Creating your blog and posting to it is only half the fun. When you log in to **www.blogger.com** with your Google Account, any blogs you have created will be displayed in the Dashboard. The four tabs seen at the top of the screen (Posting, Settings, Layout, and View Blog) let you control your blog.

WHY IT'S IMPORTANT

- **Control the content of blog posts**

  With the Posting tab, you can edit the posting of others. This is important because as the administrator of the blog, you can control whose postings become public. This means you can control the use of profanity or negative comments on your blog.

- **Use Settings to control a blog**

  The Settings tab contains eight subtabs: Basic, Publishing, Formatting, Comments, Archiving, Site Feed, Email, and Permissions. The following list contains some of what you can do with the Settings tab:
  - **Basic:** Display your blog in **blogger.com** so others may see your blog and allow search engines to find your blog.
  - **Publishing:** Change the address of your blog.
  - **Formatting:** Change the number of posts that are displayed, the date and time-stamp format, and the language in which your blog is displayed.
  - **Comments:** Determine who can comment and whether you want to moderate the comments. See Figure B-14.
  - **Archiving:** Determines how often the blog is archived.
  - **Site Feed:** Determines how much of each post is automatically displayed.
  - **Email:** Sets up an address that automatically notifies you when someone publishes to your blog.
  - **Permissions:** Determines who can post to the blog, and who has Administrator status.

- **Arrange elements on the page**

  With the Layout tab, you can modify the various options of the template you use. The Page Elements tab, shown in Figure B-15, lets you add and arrange elements on the page. Use the Fonts and Colors tab, shown in Figure B-16, to change the colors used in the blog page. The upper pane contains controls that let you change colors in your blog page. As you click a selection, the corresponding color in the blog page sample changes instantly showing you the new effect. When you click the Pop Out link, the sample area enlarges and the controls move to their own window. You can always see how your blog looks by clicking the View Blog tab.

MODIFYING AN EXISTING BLOG

You'd like to spice up your family blog. You've decided to add photos and change settings to make it more appealing.

1. **Point your browser to www.blogger.com and log in to your Google Account, if necessary**
2. **Open your family blog, click the Layout tab, then click the Page Elements tab, if necessary**
3. **Rearrange at least two elements on the page**
4. **Add at least one element to the page**
5. **Preview and save your changes, then return to the Dashboard**

FIGURE B-14: Comments subtab on Settings tab

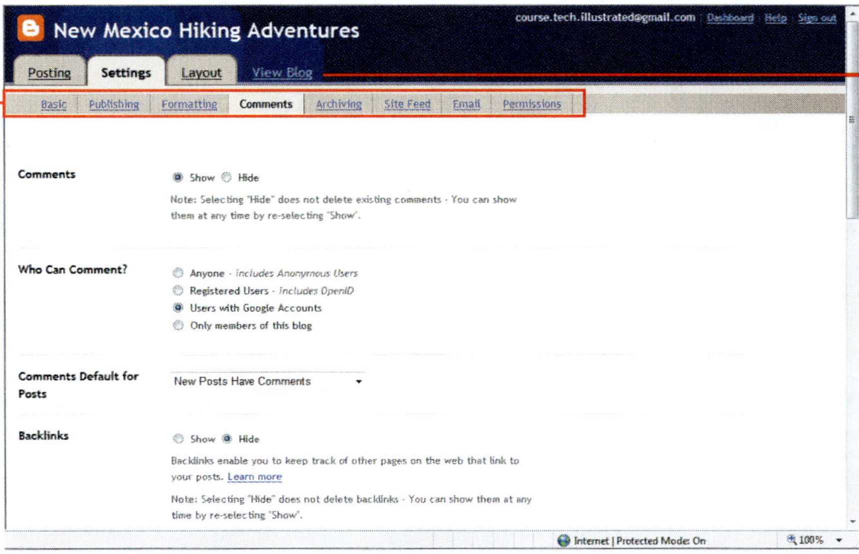

FIGURE B-15: Add and Arrange Page Elements

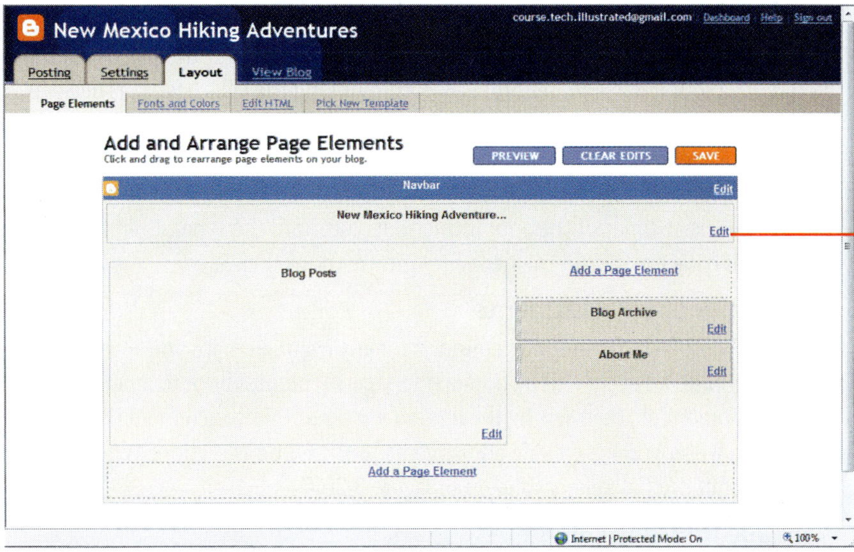

FIGURE B-16: Fonts and Colors subtab in Layout tab

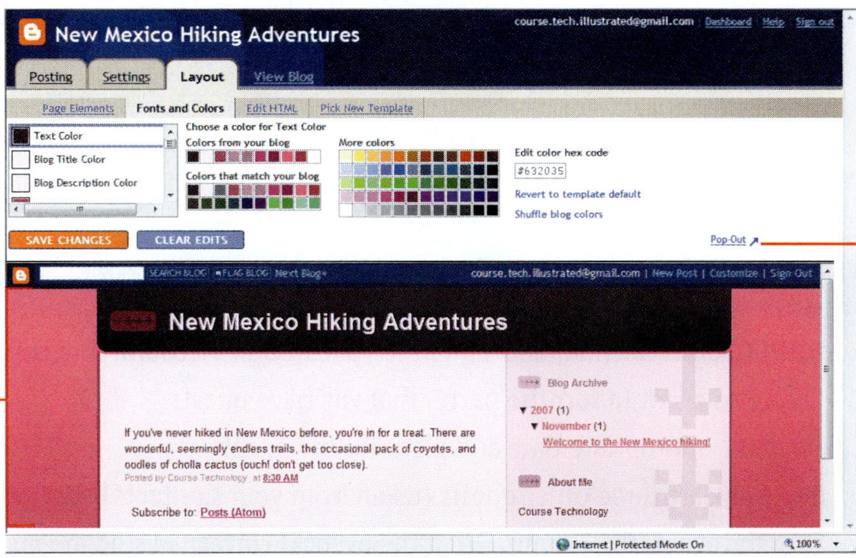

Google

UNIT
B
Google

Making Appointments with Google Calendar

The **Google Calendar** lets you keep track of your appointments (known as events) and lets you include others in these events. Google Calendar also lets you create multiple calendars or import calendars created in other file formats. You can open Google Calendar by pointing your browser to **www.google.com/calendar**, clicking the Calendar link from Gmail, or by clicking the more link from the Google search page, then clicking Calendar.

WHY IT'S IMPORTANT

QUICK TIP
You can create an event for the next day that has no guests by clicking the Quick Add link. You might use this feature as a reminder to yourself to stop at the grocery store or mail a letter.

- **Schedule events**
  With Calendar, you will always know where you're supposed to be. You can use Calendar for important business appointments or mundane tasks that you don't want to forget. When you open Calendar, you can advance to any date. The calendar will display the days of the week (by default) as well as a small monthly calendar, as shown in Figure B-17. The calendar view can be changed by clicking a tab for a Day, Week, Month, or for the Next 4 Days. Calendar events can also be viewed in a list using the Agenda tab. When you create an event, the information is entered in the calendar on the dates and times you specify. The people you invite (your guests) are sent messages announcing the event, which they can accept, decline, or propose a new time. The event information is then sent to the calendar on their computer (even if they are not using Gmail). For each response to your invitation, you will receive an acknowledgement of the response. You can create an event by clicking the Create Event link. The Create Event screen, shown in Figure B-18, lets you specify the exact times of the appointment, its location, the type of reminder you want, and the attendees. When you have entered all the necessary information, click Save.

QUICK TIP
A reminder can be a pop-up message and/or e-mail and can be scheduled up to one week in advance.

- **Keep track of appointments**
  You can choose to have multiple reminders for any event. Perhaps you want to be reminded by e-mail message one day prior to an event and by pop-up message 10 minutes prior to an event. You can do this by clicking the Add a reminder link, then setting the reminder type and time increment list arrows as desired. See Figure B-19. Click Save when you have made adjustments to the Options section. When you have finished your event, it will appear in the Calendar, as shown in Figure B-20.

QUICK TIP
Click the Sync with Microsoft Outlook Calendar link to upload a utility program that lets you integrate data from Microsoft Outlook and Gmail calendars.

- **Manage multiple calendars**
  Even though you're only one person, events in your life might demand more than one calendar. You might want multiple calendars to manage events in your personal life versus events in your professional life. In most cases, a calendar would be created for your own use, but you might want to create a calendar that can be shared with other users. A calendar can be shared with everyone, or with specific people you designate. After you click Add, then click the Create a new calendar link, you can determine who can share your calendar. A Public calendar is one that contains information from an outside source, such as Netflix, and can be added to your own calendar.

CREATING AN APPOINTMENT

You and several friends are planning a surprise party for a colleague. You've decided to use Google Calendar to keep everyone current as to the date and time of the event.

1. **Open Google Calendar and sign in to your Google Account, if necessary**
2. **Create an event (a surprise party) that will have guests**
3. **Fill in the appropriate time and place for the event**
4. **Invite at least three other guests (taken from your Contacts list)**
5. **Save the event, then confirm that the event is correctly listed in your calendar**

FIGURE B-17: Google Calendar

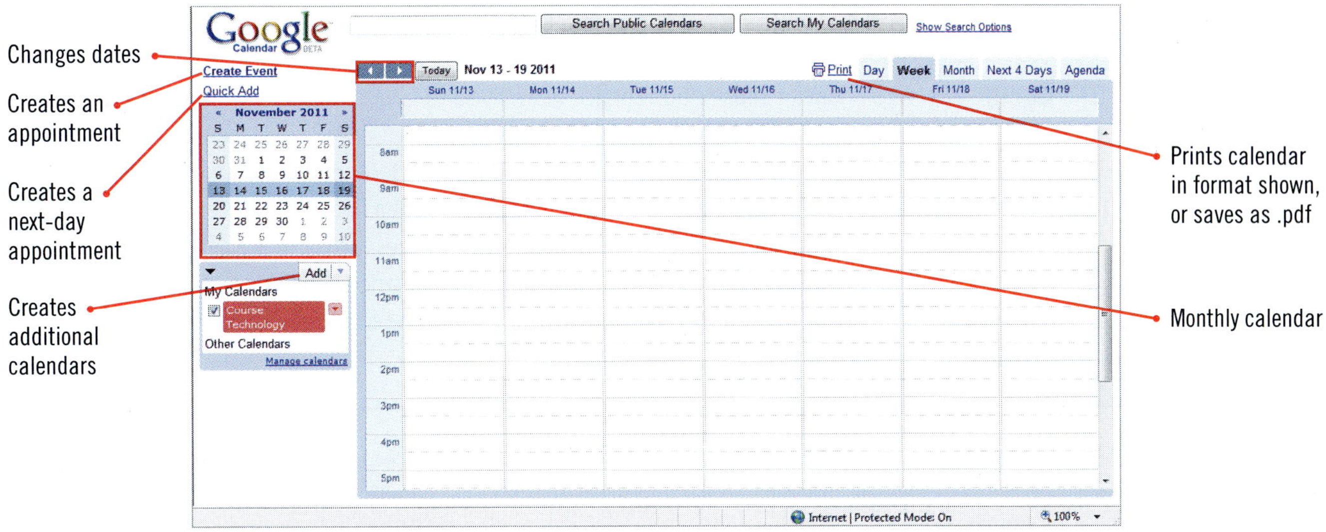

FIGURE B-18: Event specifications

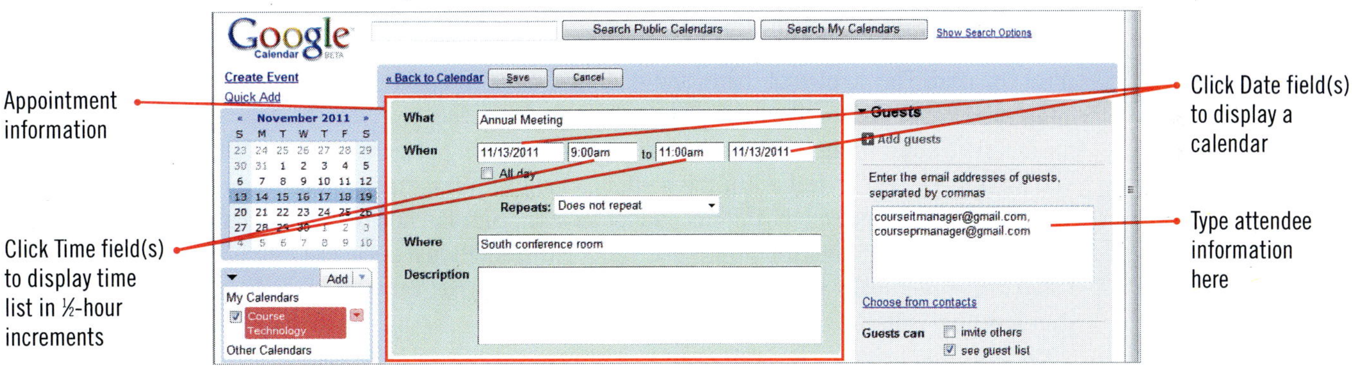

FIGURE B-19: Options in Google Calendar

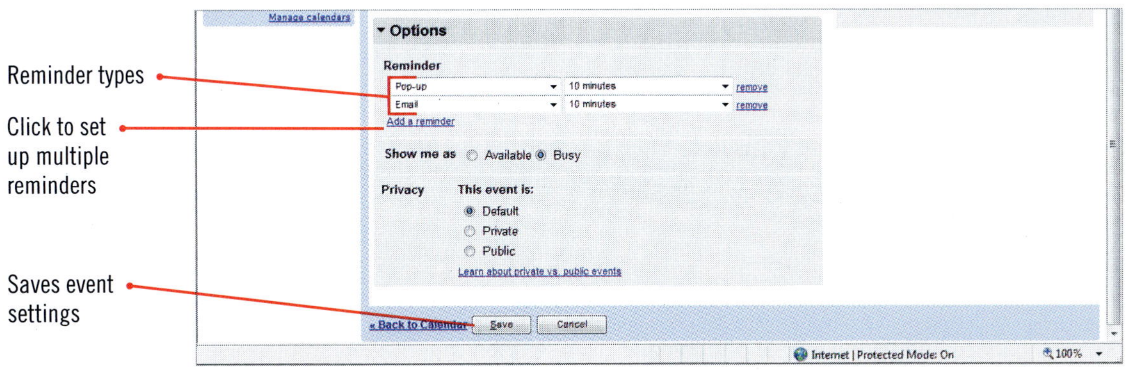

FIGURE B-20: Event in Google Calendar

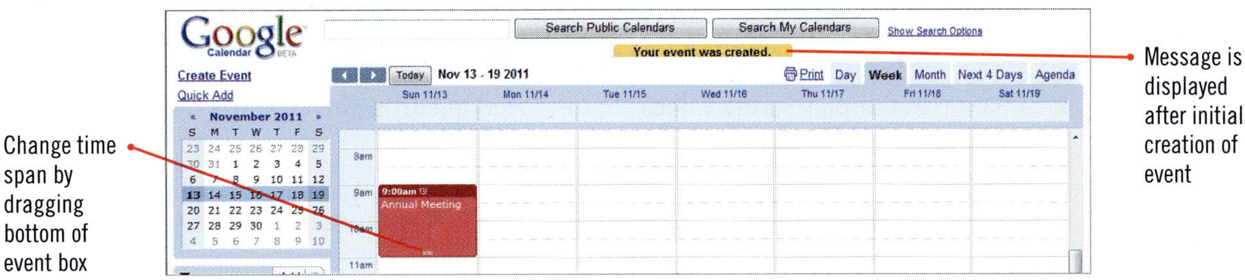

Google

UNIT B

Google

Tracking Financial Assets

The **Google Finance** financial information service allows you to create multiple portfolios to keep track of your financial assets. The initial Google Finance page is shown in Figure B-21 and is updated every 10 minutes (with a 20-minute delay). Beneath the Recent quotes and Related news areas are links to news on Top movers, Today's news, a Sector summary, and video links to news of a financial nature. News feeds relevant to entries in your portfolio are included in this area. This page makes it easy to always have an at-a-glance overview of your financial assets. You can open Google Finance by clicking more from the Google menu, then clicking Finance, or by pointing your browser to **finance.google.com**.

WHY IT'S IMPORTANT

QUICK TIP

Positive values are displayed in green; negative values are displayed in red.

- **Create your own portfolio**

  Everyone's assets are different, so it's important that you are able to easily create and maintain your own portfolio. You can create a portfolio by clicking the Portfolios link either at the upper right of the screen or above the sample of Recent quotes. You can give each of your portfolios meaningful names, such as Retirement planning, Assets for Anniversary trip, or New baby education fund. Now that you've named your portfolio, it's time to add assets to it. Each portfolio can contain an unlimited number of assets. You can enter stock symbols (or tickers) into the empty portfolio as well as the number of shares you own and the price you paid. The number of shares and the initial price you paid is optional, but the more information you enter, the better the financial picture your portfolio will give you. As you type characters in the Symbol(s) text box, similar tickers will be displayed, as shown in Figure B-22. Click the symbol of the stock you want and it will be entered in the portfolio along with the financial board from which it originates. When you have entered all the information for an asset, click the Add to portfolio button. The asset will be displayed in the portfolio with the last price, along with additional calculated information, such as the cost basis (what you initially paid for the shares), the current market value, the overall gain/loss, and the daily gain/loss. See Figure B-23.

QUICK TIP

Get detailed information about a specific asset in your portfolio by clicking its name or symbol.

- **Maintain your portfolio**

  Financial data is always changing, and it's unrealistic to think that the assets you own today will be the same ones you own in a day, week, month, or year. You can always add assets to your portfolio by entering stocks and clicking the Add to portfolio button. Remove an asset or change the data you've entered for it by clicking the Edit transactions link. Click the Edit portfolio link to change the portfolio name, the default currency in which the values are displayed, or the order in which the assets are listed. If you are keeping detailed data records of your financial assets, you can download the transactions to a spreadsheet by clicking the Download to spreadsheet link. A file in a format readable by Google Docs and Microsoft Excel will be created that you can use in your favorite spreadsheet program.

CREATING A PORTFOLIO

You have been putting off understanding your financial position and have decided that it's time to organize your assets.

1. **Point your browser to finance.google.com, then log in with your Google Account, if necessary**
2. **Create a portfolio with a name that's meaningful to you**
3. **Add at least three assets that you really do own, or would like to purchase**
4. **Change the display so the values are displayed in Euros, then change the default currency back to United States Dollar**

FIGURE B-21: Google Finance

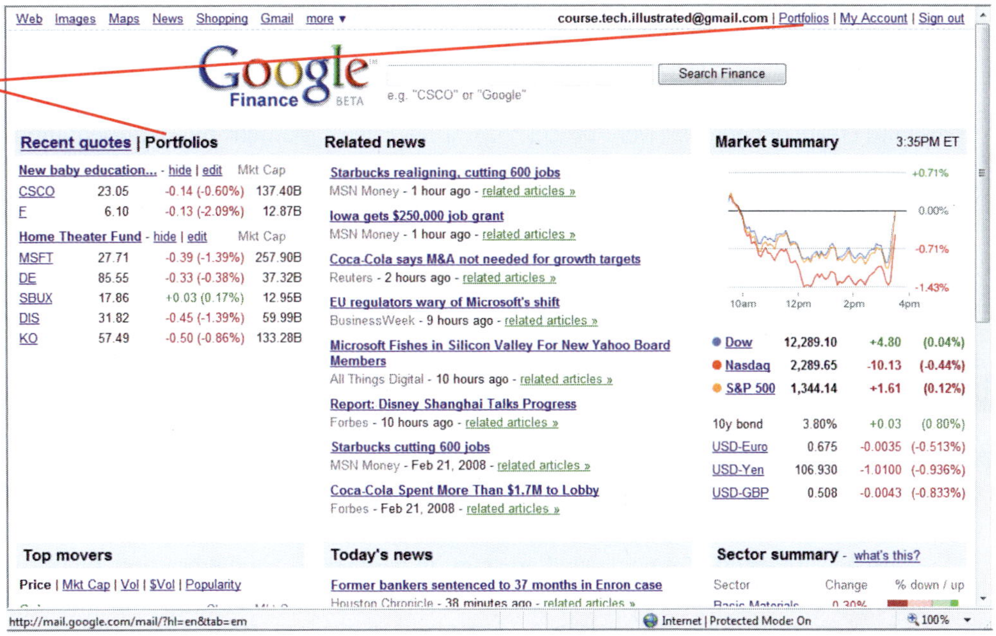

FIGURE B-22: Entering an asset

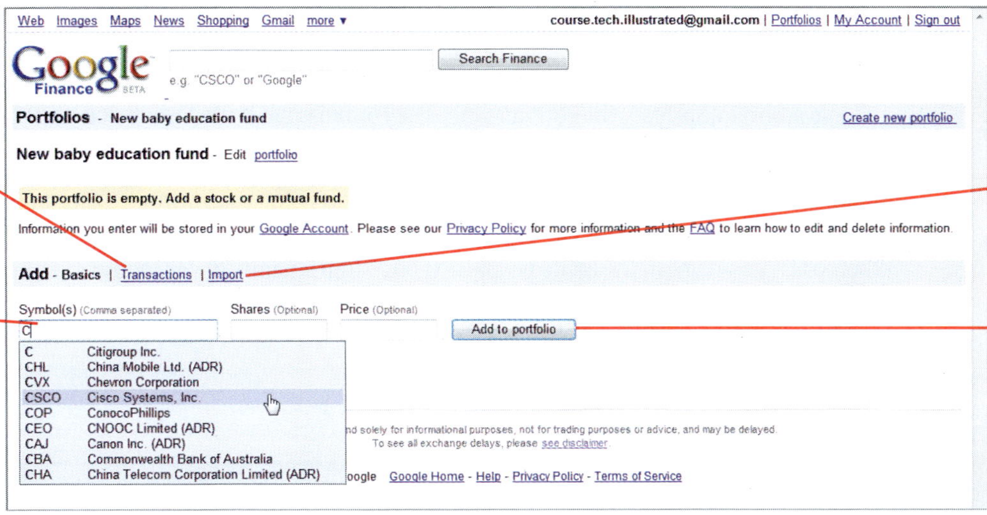

FIGURE B-23: Portfolio with assets

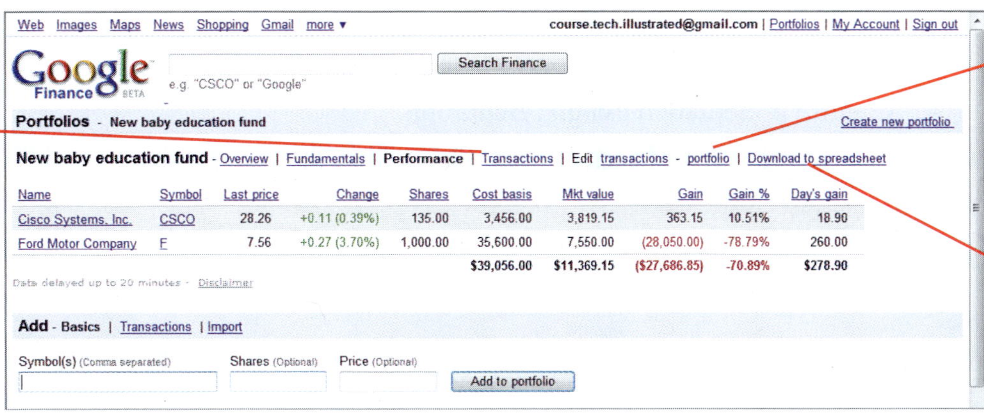

UNIT
B
Google

Using Google Docs

Google Docs word processing and spreadsheet program is Web-based application software that can be used to create documents (word processing), spreadsheets (numeric data), presentations (text and graphics in a slide format), or file folders (used to organize your files). Files created by Google Docs can be read and modified by other commonly used business application software programs. If you already know how to create these types of files, you'll have no trouble creating them in Google Docs. You can open Google Docs by clicking the Documents link in either the Gmail or Google Calendar screens, or by pointing your browser to **docs.google.com**.

WHY IT'S IMPORTANT

QUICK TIP
You can open an existing file by clicking its name.

- ### Create important business documents

  Like many other Google programs, Google Docs is Web based, which means that it doesn't take up any room on your computer's hard drive and can be accessed from any computer with an active Internet connection. The most commonly used programs in business are word processing, spreadsheets, and presentation graphics. Google Docs lets you create all three file types, using icons and formatting rules commonly found in its much more expensive competitors. Figure B-24 displays the initial Google Docs screen in which three files have been created. The icon for each file indicates the type of file it is (word processing, spreadsheet, or presentation).

  - You can create a new Google Docs file by clicking the New button on the menu bar, then selecting Document, Spreadsheet, or Presentation. A new file window is displayed over the Google Docs window.
  - You can save your file by clicking Save, as shown in Figure B-25. If you've ever used any word processor, the buttons in the editing toolbar might look familiar to you. Figure B-26 shows a Google Docs spreadsheet displaying the Formulas tab. The Formulas tab is used when you want to create formulas.

QUICK TIP
If you hold the mouse pointer over a button, a ScreenTip is displayed that identifies its function.

- ### Share files with others

  Any file created using Google Docs can be kept exclusively for your own use or can be shared with other users. To share a file, click the Share tab, then click the Invite collaborators link to invite others to use a file. When you type a name in the Invite people text box, similar names in your address book are displayed, making selection easy.

CREATING BUSINESS FILES

You have been put in charge of creating files needed for the quarterly sales meeting and you will need a cover letter, a summary of sales from each corporate division, and a presentation that summarizes sales progress in each division. You decide to use Google Docs to create these files.

1. **Open Google Docs and log in to your Google Account, if necessary**
2. **Create a cover letter using Documents**
3. **Create a spreadsheet using Spreadsheets**
4. **Create a presentation using Presentation**
5. **Change the status of each of these files so that they can be shared**

FIGURE B-24: Google Docs

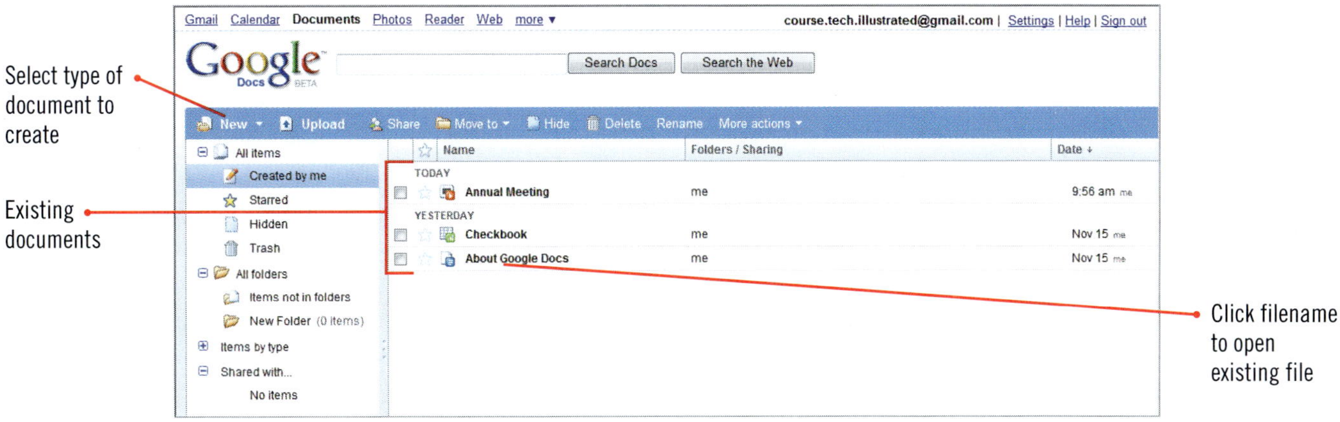

FIGURE B-25: Document in Google Docs

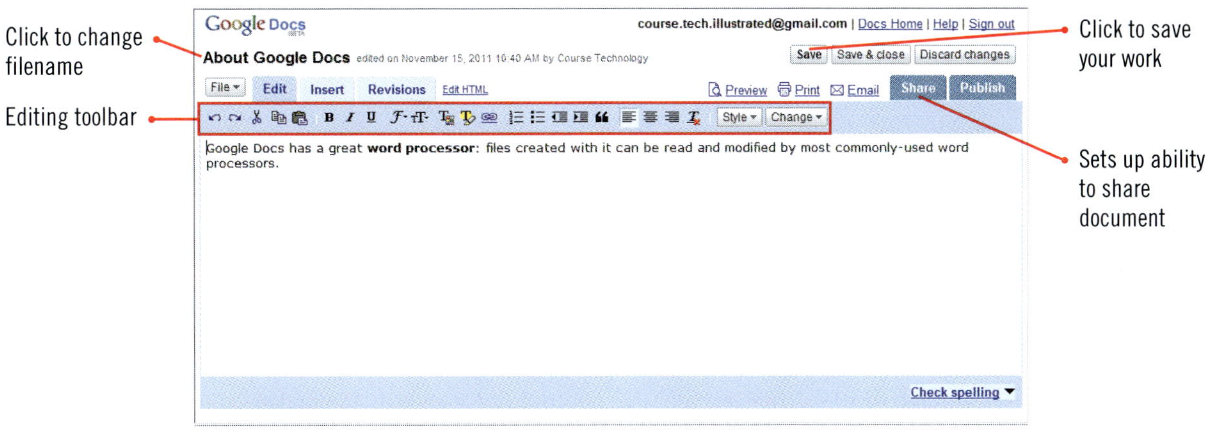

FIGURE B-26: Spreadsheet in Google Docs

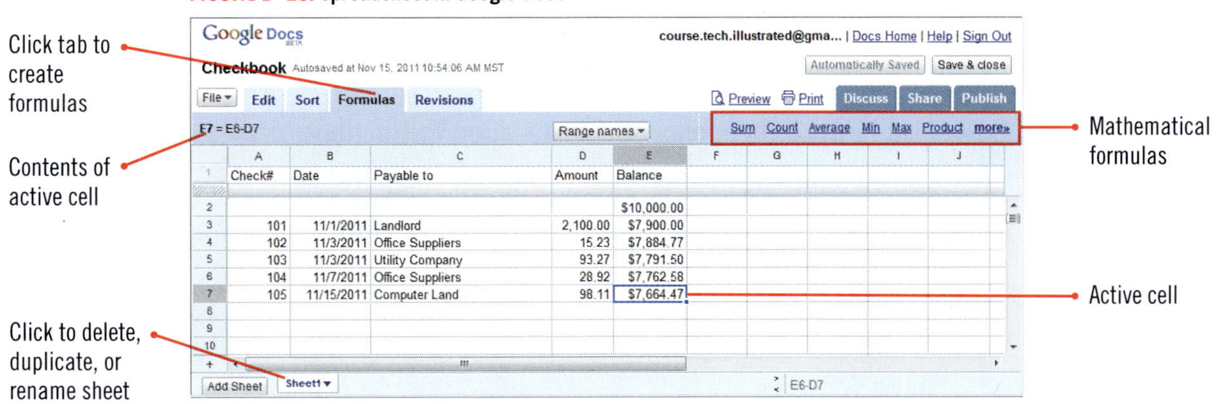

Managing Images with Picasa

Picasa (sometimes called Picasa2) photo organizing software is a program that allows you to organize and edit digital images. Picasa must be downloaded and installed on your computer. With Picasa, you can make image corrections for contrast and color, cropping and straightening, highlights, shadows, color temperature, and a variety of color tint effects. You can also use Picasa to export, order prints, post to the Web, print, e-mail, and create collages. **Picasa Web Albums** is a companion Web-based program that allows you to post, share, and organize photos on the Web. Access the Picasa download by pointing your browser to **picasa.google.com**, then clicking the Try Picasa Now link and following the download instructions. Open the Picasa Web Album by pointing your browser to **picasaweb.google.com**.

WHY IT'S IMPORTANT

QUICK TIP
Remember to check the copyright of any image you acquire from the Internet.

- **Organize images on your computer**
  With Picasa, you can create multiple albums containing any number of images. These images can be displayed on your computer monitor as a slide show, packaged on a CD, or posted to a universally available Web site. Within albums, you can rearrange images, mark them for selection, and create screen savers. Picasa can also find images that are already on your computer, or you can import them from a camera, external storage, or other sources, such as Google Images. Figure B-27 shows a sample folder within an album. Three of the images have a star in the lower-right corner, indicating that they have been marked for selection. The selection feature can be used to manipulate multiple images at once, or to selectively choose which images you want to share with others.

QUICK TIP
Mac users can use iPhoto instead of Picasa2 to complete similar tasks.

- **Edit your images**
  You can use Picasa to edit your images by making basic fixes to the image, such as cropping, straightening, removing red eye, and adjusting contrast, color, or fill light. After double-clicking an image, you can use the Basic Fixes, Tuning, or Effects tabs to make major or minor changes to an image. Table B-1 lists many of the modifications you can make using Picasa.

QUICK TIP
You can create a Picasa Web Album without installing Picasa on your computer.

- **Use a Picasa Web Album**
  After your album is ready to be displayed online, click the Web Album button, sign in using your Gmail account information, complete the Send photos to a Picasa Web Album dialog box, then click OK. You can reorder images in a Picasa Web Album by clicking the Organize button, then either dragging images to a new location or clicking the Sort photos by list arrow. To create a Web album, go to Picasa Web Albums, click the New Album link, complete the information in the Create a new album dialog box, then click Create. Click the Upload Photos link, then click the Add Photos link. Navigate the Open dialog box to find the images you want to add, then Open. Once all the images are displayed in the Upload Photos to dialog box, click Upload. Click the Share Album button shown in Figure B-28 to make an album available to others. Invitees receive an e-mail invitation containing a link they click that allows them to open and view the album.

CREATING A PHOTO ALBUM

You are preparing for a presentation that will require the participation of multiple team members located throughout the country. You and your teammates need to work together using Web tools to decide which images to use.

1. **Download Picasa2, then follow the installation instructions**
2. **Create an album using images already on your computer**
3. **Create a contact sheet using at least three of the images. E-mail the contact sheet to your instructor**
4. **Send an invitation to view your album to your instructor and at least one other person**

FIGURE B-27: Picasa Album

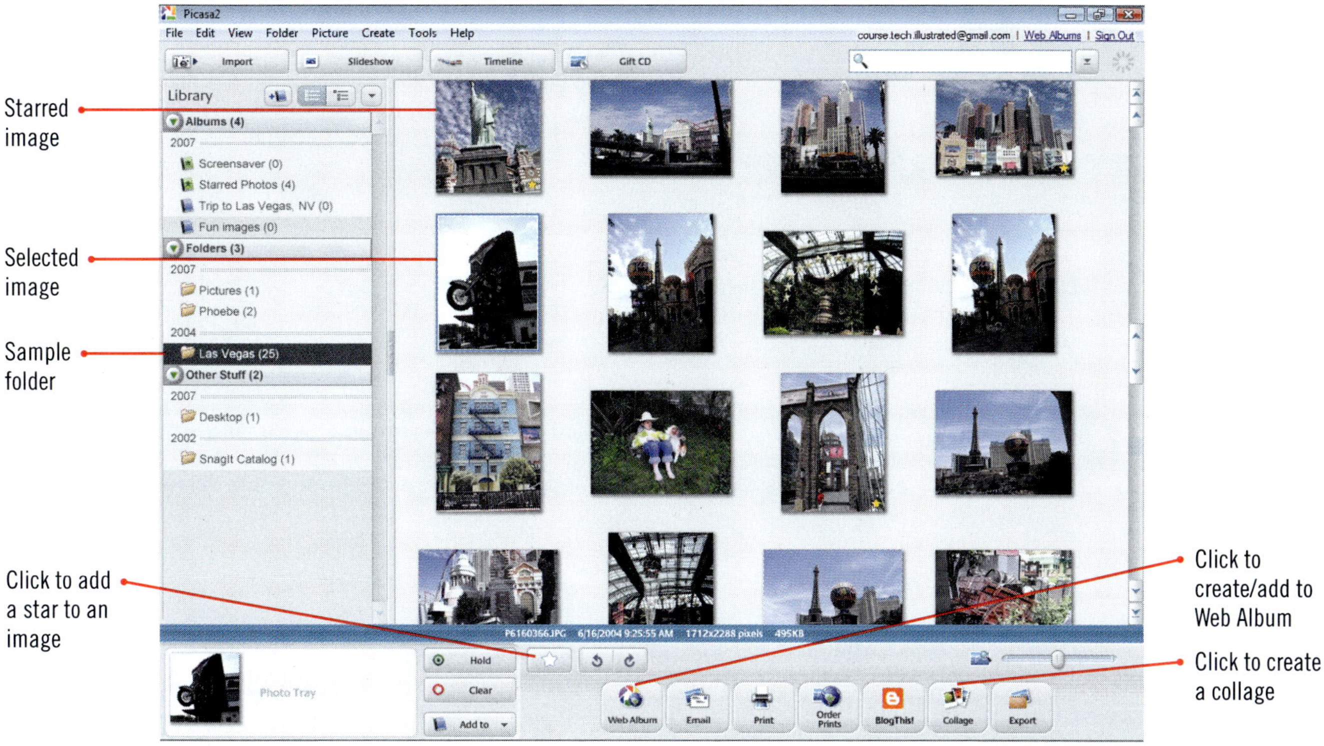

FIGURE B-28: Picasa Web Album

TABLE B-1: Possible image modifications using Picasa

tabs	tools
basic fixes	Crop, Straighten, Redeye, Auto Contrast, Auto Color, Fill Light
tuning	Fill Light, Highlights, Shadows, Color Temperature, Neutral Color Picker
effects	Sharpen, Sepia, B&W, Warmify, Film Grain, Tint, Saturation, Soft Focus, Glow, Filtered B&W, Focal B&W, Graduated Tint

Practice

If you have a SAM user profile, you may have access to hands-on instruction, practice, and assessment of the skills covered in this unit. Log in to your SAM account (http://sam2007.course.com/) to launch any assigned training activities or exams that relate to the skills covered in this unit.

▼ CONCEPTS REVIEW

Label the use of the elements shown in Figure B-29.

FIGURE B-29

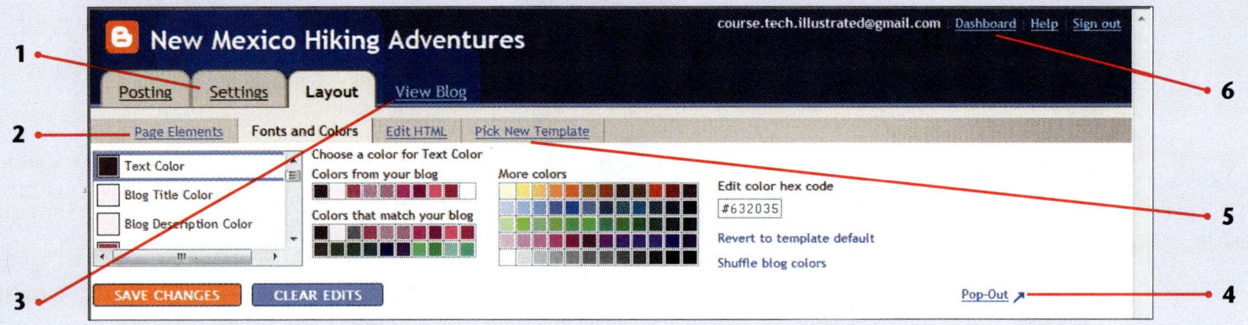

Match each Google program with the statement that best describes it.

7. Gmail
8. Calendar
9. Docs
10. Picasa
11. Blogger
12. Finance

a. Create appointments and track events
b. Manage images and photo albums
c. Track financial assets
d. Send and reply to messages
e. Create word processing, spreadsheets, and presentations
f. Create and participate in blogs

Select the best answer from the list of choices.

13. Which Gmail feature sends a copy to a recipient, but hides the recipient's name from all but the sender?
a. Add Cc
b. Add event invitation
c. Add Bcc
d. None of the above

14. Which Google program accesses public online forums?
a. Talk
b. Groups
c. iGoogle
d. Docs

15. Which of the following contains valid Google Calendar views?
a. Day, Week, Month
b. Day, Next 4 Days, Month
c. Work Week, Week, Month
d. Day, Month, Year

16. The Google Calendar Quick Add feature lets you create what type of event?
a. One that takes place the next day with no guests
b. One that takes place in two days with no guests
c. One that takes place the next day with one guest
d. One that takes place the same day with one guest

17. Which Google program shows you the number of forums by topic?
a. Google Talk
b. Blogger
c. Google Groups
d. Google Calendar

18. Which Google programs can be installed on your computer and/or run from a Web site?

- **a.** Picasa and Groups
- **b.** Gmail and Google Calendar
- **c.** Google Talk and Gmail
- **d.** Picasa and Google Talk

19. Which statement about Blogger is true?

- **a.** You can create and customize your own blog.
- **b.** You can rearrange elements in your blog.
- **c.** All your blogs are displayed in the Dashboard area.
- **d.** All of the above

20. Which Google program lets you communicate instantly with other Google users?

- **a.** Google Picasa
- **b.** Google Calendar
- **c.** Google Share
- **d.** Google Talk

21. Google Finance shows you:

- **a.** Financial news relevant to assets in your portfolio.
- **b.** Financial and entertainment news.
- **c.** Assets similar to those in your portfolio.
- **d.** News about assets you owned previously.

22. Which statement about Google Finance is true?

- **a.** Each portfolio can contain up to 25 assets.
- **b.** Your portfolio is updated every 10 minutes.
- **c.** Portfolio assets can only be displayed in U.S. dollars.
- **d.** Declining prices are shown in blue.

▼ INDEPENDENT CHALLENGE 1

You have been asked to assemble a team of expert Google users to train others in your company. Each member of your team will be asked to make a trip to Washington, D.C., to lead a training class in the use of Google programs.

- **a.** Point your browser to Gmail, and log in to your account, if necessary.
- **b.** Enter at least three colleagues (you can use classmates, other friends, or fictitious names) as Gmail contacts.
- **c.** Create a nonrepeating calendar appointment for each of the three colleagues (using your date of birth this year as their training date).
- **d.** Include a pop-up reminder one day before the event occurs, compare your appointment event with Figure B-30, then save the event.
- **d.** Use Google Talk to have an online chat session with each of the team members to let them know about the upcoming event.
- **e.** Print the page, compare your results with Figure B-31, then exit Google Calendar.

FIGURE B-30

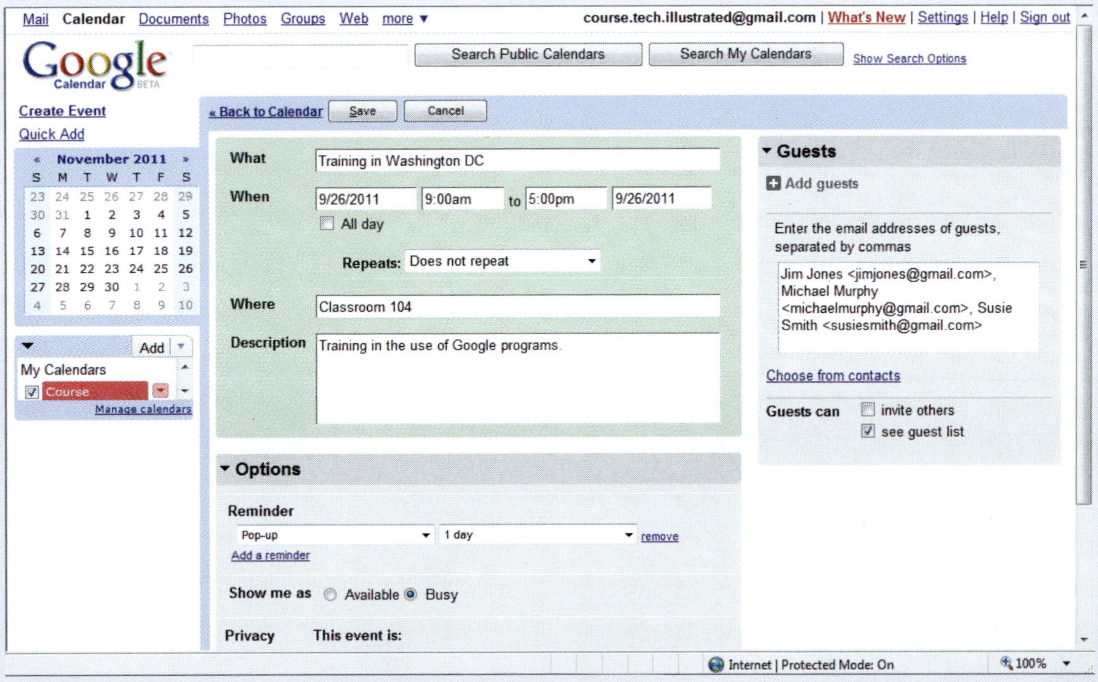

▼ INDEPENDENT CHALLENGE 2

You have always been interested in technology, but some topics confuse you more than others, such as television broadcast in high definition. You've decided to create a blog about an important aspect of technology that you need to understand better.

- **a.** Point your browser to Blogger, and log in to your account, if necessary.
- **b.** Choose a name for your blog, then choose a template.
- **c.** Create an initial post for your blog.
- **d.** Send an invitation to at least three of your classmates, notifying them that you'd like them to participate in your blog.
- **e.** Compare your blog with the one shown in Figure B-31, then exit Blogger.

FIGURE B-31

▼ VISUAL WORKSHOP

Use Table B-2 to create a portfolio called **Home Theater Fund** using Google Finance, then download the portfolio to a spreadsheet. See Figure B-32 (your calculated values will be different). (*Hint*: The contents of column A may be truncated.) Print the spreadsheet and submit it to your instructor without saving it.

TABLE B-2

Name	Symbol	Shares
Microsoft Corporation	MSFT	52
Deere & Company	DE	246
Starbucks Corporation	SBUX	900
The Walt Disney Company	DIS	17
The Coca-Cola Company	KO	1500

FIGURE B-32

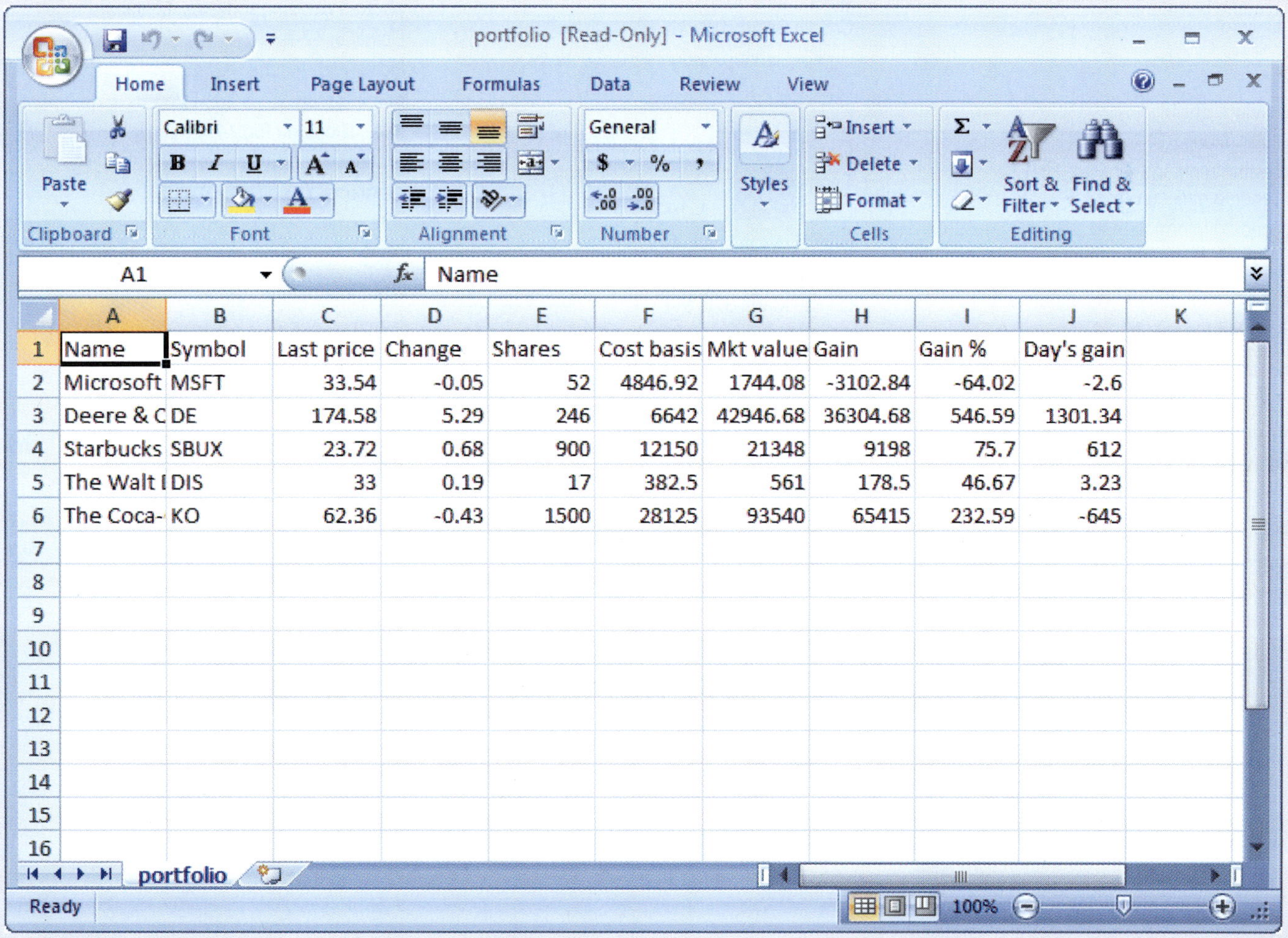

	A	B	C	D	E	F	G	H	I	J	K
1	Name	Symbol	Last price	Change	Shares	Cost basis	Mkt value	Gain	Gain %	Day's gain	
2	Microsoft	MSFT	33.54	-0.05	52	4846.92	1744.08	-3102.84	-64.02	-2.6	
3	Deere & C	DE	174.58	5.29	246	6642	42946.68	36304.68	546.59	1301.34	
4	Starbucks	SBUX	23.72	0.68	900	12150	21348	9198	75.7	612	
5	The Walt I	DIS	33	0.19	17	382.5	561	178.5	46.67	3.23	
6	The Coca-	KO	62.36	-0.43	1500	28125	93540	65415	232.59	-645	

Index